30 Things

30 Things

Practical Advice
for Living Well

William H. Schaberg

Rebellion Dogs Publishing

Copyright © 2024 William H. Schaberg
All rights reserved. No portion of this book may be reproduced in any form or by any electronic or mechanical means, including information storage and retrieval systems, without the written consent of the publisher. Not sure? Please contact the publisher for permission.

    Rebellion Dogs Publishing
    Toronto, Canada
    1-416-239-8737
    news@rebelliondogspublishing.com
    https://rebelliondogspublishing.com

ISBN: 978-0-9881157-4-3 (Hardcover with Dust-jacket)
           978-0-9881157-6-7 (Hardcover Laminate)
           978-0-9881157-3-6 (Paperback)
           978-0-9881157-5-0 (Ebook)

for
Lucy Rose DaSilva
(heart of my heart)

and
My Lady Sara
(who owns that heart)

Doesn't everything die at last, and too soon?
Tell me, what is it you plan to do
with your one wild and precious life?

>   Mary Oliver
>   *The Summer Day*

Contents

	Introduction	i
1.	Loving Someone	1
2.	Business Success	5
3.	Communication	9
4.	New Habits	13
5.	Pretending?	17
6.	Insufficient Data	21
7.	Never Say	25
8.	Pay Attention	29
9.	Universally Different	35
10.	Emotional Coward	39
11.	Five Things	43
12.	Spiritual Encounters	47
13.	Experiential Truth	51
14.	The Cauldron	55
15.	Transparency	59
16.	Compassion	63
17.	Newfound Clarity	67
18.	Standing Where?	71
19.	Future-Back Planning	75
20.	Poetry	79

21.	Welcome!	85
22.	Cash Value	89
23.	Constitutionally Incapable	95
24.	The Morning	101
25.	Only You	107
26.	First Conversation	113
27.	Skillfulness	117
28.	Doing Something	123
29.	Trend Lines	129
30.	Meditation	135

Introduction

THE IDEA FOR this book came to me while I was reading a newspaper article.

One of my favorite writers for the *New York Times* invited readers to send him examples of "The Best Advice You've Ever Received (and Are Willing to Pass On)".

On June 10, 2019, they printed the twenty-five best entries he had received.

I was captivated by the premise and the promise of this article and eagerly began to read what I expected to be some really helpful pieces of advice. Alas... I could not have been more disappointed. What had been selected as "best" struck me as either trivial ("Take a breath"), obvious ("When you go in to a job interview, have questions ready") or downright pointless (You've never seen a dead cat in a tree, have you?").

Really? Those are best examples selected from what I suspected must have been several hundred (if not a few thousand) submissions?

My immediate reaction was to remember some of the great advice I had received over the years – suggestions that were far more valuable and life-enhancing than anything the *Times* had just published.

Our world is full of advice. Some of it comes from friends and relatives – occasionally when we ask for it, and at other times, when we don't. Advice is also regularly offered by teachers, religious leaders, employers, therapists and motivational speakers. In addition, a wealth of excellent suggestions can be found in the many articles and books offering various and sundry ways to improve our lives.

Maybe I've been extremely lucky, but I've always been blessed with great friends – understanding and genuinely caring people, many of whom have a talent for delivering helpful advice in such a way that I can actually *hear* it. *(That is to say they typically offer their advice in a "this is what worked for me" format rather than in the more directive "this is what you should be doing" style.)*

Besides those friends, I have been a lifelong reader and spiritual seeker so I've been exposed to some truly amazing teachers – in person, on recordings and in print – teachers who have regularly helped guide me in the right direction.

Finally, a few of these "30 Things" came from my own experiences (both positive and negative) which evolved into suggestions that I have felt comfortable offering to others – when asked and when appropriate – because they have proven to be so beneficial for me personally.

It is a truism that the older we get, the more we tend to repeat ourselves... with discouraging regularity!

Caught out in these situations more frequently than I care to admit, I have often defended myself by saying: "Well, you know, I've only got about thirty worthwhile things to say, so please stop me if you've heard me say this before..."

My disappointment with the *Times* article prompted me to take that rather lame excuse a bit more seriously and I set out to write down some of those "thirty worthwhile things." The general format I've tried to use here is to tell the story of how I first heard each piece of advice and then provide some examples of the way it has actually made a difference in my life.

I must honestly admit that, at first glance, some of these suggestions struck me as downright crazy or – to put it more positively – as seriously counter-intuitive.

But contrary advice is frequently far more helpful than the familiar bromides and pious platitudes that people so often offer (such as "Be a Gentleman" – another one of the *Times* winners!). By their very definition, bromides are comfortable and palatable, rarely calling for any kind of specific or significant change in our behavior.

In contrast, unconventional wisdom is all too often challenging, demanding and uncomfortable.

But, however crazy or counter-intuitive some of this advice may have sounded to me at first, it all resonated on a more primal level. While my head insisted on posing contrary arguments, my stomach knew this was something I should be paying attention to and, perhaps, even trying to put into practice.

And, to the best of my abilities, I have done that.

All of the different pieces of advice offered here have worked for me – really worked for me to one degree or another – in so far as I was willing to honestly try to incorporate them into my life.

Admittedly, there is no universal, one-size-fits-all set of answers to the myriad challenges we all face as we try to successfully navigate our way through life.

But each of these "30 Things" has helped me with my ongoing efforts to "live well".

Perhaps some of them will be helpful for you too!

1.

"Loving someone means acting as if their happiness is important to you"

THAT IS PROBABLY the single most important piece of advice I've ever heard – and then put into practice.

I was listening to a motivational talk by a man named Paul – (in the world before podcasts, we had cassette tapes and I listened to hundreds of them while driving!) – and he was telling this extremely long story about how he gets up before his wife every morning and goes downstairs to make her a cup of coffee.

It had to be her favorite kind of coffee, he said, served in her favorite cup. The beans had to be carefully measured and then ground (just so!) before he poured in the water – having been brought to the perfect "rolling" boil. To this, he added just the right amount of cream (not milk... and no sugar!). Once that was all done, the final step was to add an ice cube of exactly the right size – one that would have just melted as he climbed the stairs and carefully placed the cup on his wife's bedside table. Paul said he would then stir the coffee to make sure that it was at a uniform and perfectly drinkable temperature.

His wife would wake up and nod appreciatively as she reached for the cup.

I swear that story was five-minutes long and I couldn't for the life of me figure out why I was listening to all of these excruciating details.

Then Paul said: "The reason I'm telling you this story is to make a point. And the point is that loving someone means *acting* as if their happiness is important to you."

He stressed that word "*acting*" pretty emphatically.

This hit me so hard that I pulled the car over to the side of road and wrote it down.

I have been blessed with an amazing relationship with a fabulous woman – my wife, the Lady Sara – and, to tell the truth, we had actually been doing something along those lines in our home for some time before I heard Paul's story.

But, to be perfectly honest, Sara was far more devoted to acting as if my happiness was important to her, than I was to holding up my side of that bargain.

And I knew this was absolutely true the second I heard Paul deliver his punch line.

Sara constantly paid attention to my wants and needs; always doing things for me before I asked and, sometimes, before I even thought of them. It wasn't just the clean, folded clothes that materialized with such regularity. It was also the fact that menus were planned and executed with my tastes in mind. Or that a fresh pound of my favorite coffee beans would materialize in the kitchen cabinet just as the old one neared empty. And, when I wasn't feeling well, that tapioca pudding (my favorite 'comfort food') would be made without me ever mentioning it. Or, that she would point out an article in the *New Yorker* that I just "had" to read – because she knew I would enjoy it. And that she so generously made time for me to do what I wanted to do, rather than always insisting on doing what she wanted to do.

That and so... *so*... SO much more.

And the truly embarrassing fact – which Paul's story rubbed my nose in so effectively – was that while all of this was happening right before my eyes, I was taking most of it for granted. A lot of it didn't even 'cross my radar.' At times, I barely noticed. When I finally did come face-to-face with this complete insensitivity on my part, I was embarrassed in the extreme!

Back home, I told Sara what I had just heard on that tape and we talked about how – on some levels – that already seemed to be working pretty well for us. But I had to admit that she was doing a much better job of it than me, and going forward, I committed to pay more attention to her wants and needs – and to *act* accordingly.

Of course, it was the "pay more attention" part that turned out to be the most important thing here. Did I really know what makes Sara happy? And, was I then actually *doing* those things?

Like so many other things in life, the answers weren't so much in the big things as in the small. Was I leaving dishes in the sink? Were the dirty socks in the hamper – or on the floor in front of it? Did I make the bed this morning? Did I put the paper down so I could honestly listen to what she was saying to me? Was I on my phone the first thing in the morning... rather than paying any attention whatsoever to her?

Or more practically:

You think we should do *what*?
  SURE!
"You need me to stop what I'm doing and help you *now*?"
  GREAT!
"You want us to get a new kitten?"
  NO PROBLEM!
"You just bought yourself a new car?"
  CONGRATULATIONS!

It also meant that sometimes (and with some regularity) I had to go beyond just pure speculation about what made her happy and ask the scary question: "So... how am I doing?" (A question that more than once has resulted in me being told about some behavior she found particularly annoying and that needed to be changed.)

I don't know how this could possibly work in a house where just *one* person was trying to put the "loving someone means..." mantra into practice as a rule. But in my home – where we have *both* adopted it as a guiding principle for our behavior – it has produced a more loving, a more attentive and a far happier relationship than we have ever known before.

Thanks, Paul! That annoying long story of yours has improved my life immensely.

2.

"Find out what your boss wants... then do it"

MY FRIEND STEVE gave me this particular piece of advice and it turned out to be extremely important and helpful to me and to several other people I've shared it with.

Just out of college, Steve was hired as a junior executive at Best Buy which – compared to its later size – was then a relatively small company. He was assigned a senior executive to be his mentor and they met regularly for lunch to discuss Steve's progress and to answer whatever questions he might have about the job and his career.

At one of those early lunches, his mentor casually asked: "So, would you like to know the secret of success in business?" Steve took out his pen and paper, but the exec told him that wouldn't be necessary. The secret was short, simple and completely memorable.

"Find out what your boss wants, then do it," he said.

After hearing this singular piece of advice, Steve began to notice that following each month's business strategy meeting – in which the target goals seemed to change regularly without rhyme or reason – all he heard from the other junior execs were complaints about how ridiculous these constant changes were and how impossible it was to accommodate them all.

Steve, on the other hand, accepted his mentor's advice and made it an integral part of his daily approach to work – he was committed to doing whatever they wanted him to do. The bosses' directions on what they expected from him that month had been clear so rather than complaining or second-guessing, he just did what they had asked of him.

A couple of years later, Steve moved on to a different job with a different company. However, the sound advice he had received from that exec never left him and his ever-upward career – along with the fact that he retired very comfortably at the age of 53 – provides ample testimony to the value of this "secret of success in business" advice.

When Steve told me this, I was amazed. Why had I never realized something so obvious all by myself? Of course, doing what the boss wants is the best way to get recognition, praise and advancement!

But, once I heard it, this piece of advice moved to the front of my brain and stayed there.

As I began to apply this mantra to my own business life, I quickly realized that many of the things my boss wanted from me – and that I wanted from the people who worked for me – were often very basic and simple. Like coming in on time and putting in a full day's work. Like being a contributing member of the team rather than a perennial naysayer. Like delivering the desired results on time – and with a smile.

I think the problem many of us have with this advice is that we all too easily fall into the comforting belief that our boss is a bit "out of touch", perhaps even incompetent. On a really bad day, we may even consider them to be a complete idiot.

In addition, it seems to be a fairly common feeling among workers that they could do a better job than their boss– if *only* they were given the chance. It's certainly what I firmly believed during those twenty years I was working for my Dad in our small family business.

But once he retired and I became the person responsible for running the company, I soon realized just how challenging and nuanced the job really was and how difficult it was for me to make some of the hard decisions so necessary to keep our little company running profitably.

Finally finding myself in charge, it didn't take long for me to realize just how difficult "being the boss" actually was and what a great job my Dad had done of it. A few years later, my brother, John, confessed the same story of enlightenment to me, just a few months after he took over the company from me.

The point of this simple piece of advice is to get out of the second-guessing game, out of the judgment seat, out of the negative arena and just do what is asked of you. *That's* your job... and it is simultaneously the surest pathway to success in the company you work for.

There is, however, another side to this.

Sometimes doing what the boss wants just isn't possible.

After selling our family business to a national consolidator, I became a vice-president in that rapidly growing company. A year later, following one of our quarterly executive sessions, I came home with five specific tasks assigned to me by our Chief Operating Officer.

After a few days reflection, I realized it just wasn't going to be possible for me to get them all done in the time allowed. (The company was very big on well-defined goals coupled with concrete, time-sensitive deadlines.) I called the COO and admitted that I had bitten off more than I could chew. I told him I could accomplish any three of the five he might like, but that two of them would have to be re-assigned elsewhere. Surprisingly, he had no problem with this and immediately took two of those tasks off my plate.

This, by the way, taught me a valuable lesson about this man's particular management style. He would assign people as many tasks as possible until he discovered their breaking point – and then never pushed them past that point again. This particular boss just wanted to ensure that he was "getting the most" out of each employee and this was his way of determining what that "most" actually was.

Bosses can be like that.

p.s. If you find that, for whatever reason, you are unwilling or cannot do what your boss wants you to do – or if they are such a terrible communicator that you are never *really sure* just what it is you are supposed to be doing next – then it is clearly time to start looking for a different job.

3.

"No matter what you may think, it's always a communication problem"

AFTER ONE YEAR together, my Lady Sara and I – very much in love but having the same disagreements over and over again – went into therapy with a couple counselor named Larry. We worked with him as a couple and also individually for about two and a half years. He was one of the three smartest people I've ever met and one of the most important and influential men in my life.

At our second or third session, he asked me to summarize our problems and I recounted a short laundry list of issues in which sex and money figured prominently. He disagreed. He said that our fundamental problem – in fact, he claimed, *the* fundamental problem faced by almost all couples – was bad communication.

I disagreed pretty forcibly (he could be *very* annoying when making one of these pontifical pronouncements), but he finally told me that if I hung in there with him for a few more sessions, I would end up agreeing with him. If I didn't, he promised to give us a free session.

We never collected on that one. The man was 100% right.

After several months of hard work with him, I was appalled to realize just how dreadful – let's be honest, how virtually non-existent! – my communication skill set had been during the first 45 years of my life.

Who knew? Certainly, not me.

There were many "ah ha" moments in Larry's office (and afterwards doing 'homework'), but the one I remember best was the time he asked me to tell Sara something directly that I had started saying to him. I turned to Sara – sitting on a couch opposite me – and I told her. He then asked Sara to repeat back what she had just heard... which turned out to be *nothing* like what I thought I had said. I couldn't figure out if she was just being dense OR if she was trying to make me look bad and score some points for 'her side' in this therapy session.

Larry came over to my chair, crouched down beside me and said: "Tell me if this is what you were trying to say?" He then proceeded to talk to Sara, repackaging my statement completely. He then checked with me to see if that was the substance of what I had meant to say and I admitted that it was. He then asked Sara what she had heard and she repeated back to us exactly what I had been trying to say to her in the first place.

I heard the difference – most especially in the tone. I heard the clarity. I heard the necessary directness. I heard the honesty.

I felt like an idiot (which, on some level, I was!).

But I learned. I was really lousy at talking to Sara... and I needed to change.

The more we worked at following several of Larry's concrete suggestions on how to effectively communicate with each other, the more intimate and the happier our relationship became.

Sometime later, I discovered that this "communication problem" didn't just apply to my most intimate relationships. Once I began to pay attention, I realized it was also one of my problems at work.

I had an employee named Ben who was in charge of more than half of our small company's business, and I was not happy with the way he was running his department. I spoke with him several times about my dissatisfaction and made what I thought were useful suggestions. But nothing ever changed. I was frustrated with the whole situation and became even more angry with him.

Finally, I typed up a document clearly detailing the things I objected to, specifying exactly what had to be done differently and threatening him with termination if those changes didn't take place in a very short time frame.

Sitting across from me in the conference room, he carefully read the document then looked up and said: "This is what you want?" At that point, I wasn't really sure why he was asking such a simplistic question, but I said: "Yes, that's what needs to happen… or else!"

Ben surprised me by confidently stating: "I can do this!" and then picked up a pen to boldly sign the acknowledgment that he had read and accepted the terms of our agreement.

He then proceeded to do all the things I wanted him to do.

Clearly, all of my previous conversations with him had failed to effectively communicate my point – meaning that I needed to take some of the communication skills I was slowly developing at home and start using them in the shop as well.

Again, life got better once I started to make some changes in how I communicated with my employees.

The final story which clearly illustrates just how overlooked and surprising this "communication problem" can be is one starring our "grandson" George.

When he was five years old, his kindergarten teacher told the children what they should do if they happened to find a gun laying around.

The instructions were: #1 – Stop! #2 – Don't Touch It! #3 – Leave the Room and #4 – Tell an Adult.

George faithfully recounted this lesson when he got home and his mother was so proud that she had him tell the story to several friends over the next few days. Sara and I were at one of these recitations, but the joy went right out of his mother's face when, at the end of his story, George turned to her and brightly asked:

"Mom... what's an 'adult'?"

Talk about a communication problem!

4.

"Want to form a new habit? Try attaching it to an old one"

At one time or another, almost everyone makes the decision to adopt some new habit in the hope of improving their life.

Maybe it's something as simple as a commitment to exercise three times a week or to give up chewing gum or to finally sit down and read *War and Peace*.

And then... it never happens.

Who hasn't made a New Year's resolution with the best of intentions only to find that when February rolls around, the only thing left is the painfully lingering memory of that great promise of change? (Or... perhaps it has been conveniently and completely forgotten because the stark admission of such a personal failure is just too much to bear.)

While this piece of advice certainly doesn't apply to every new habit you might want to acquire – it won't, for instance, help you develop the habit of speaking more judiciously to your teenager – I have found that when I want to introduce some new beneficial element into my life, attaching the desired new habit to an old one has frequently worked well for me.

It is one piece of advice I regularly offer to friends who complain they "just can't seem to get started with..." – whatever it is they are trying to get started with.

More than thirty years ago, my best friend, King – another one of the three smartest and most influential people in my life – suggested that I might benefit from getting on my knees every morning and saying a prayer. I resisted this suggestion pretty vehemently, pointing out that I had no faith whatsoever in the efficacy of "petitioning the Lord with prayer."

"No problem," he said. "It's not really the praying part that counts... it's the getting on your knees part that's important. It's about daily assuming a position of humility in relation to those things that have a significant influence and impact on your life – whatever those things might be in your particular belief system."

King told me I could foregoe "the praying part" and just do some "morning affirmations" instead. But he insisted it was important for me to do those affirmations on my knees.

I reluctantly agreed to this but I quickly found I had a really hard time remembering to do it every day. Most mornings, I was in such a big rush that I would simply 'forget' to get on my knees.

A couple of weeks later, when he asked me about my progress with this new habit, I complained about how hard it was to remember to do this every morning and, in my own defense, I insisted that it wasn't easy to acquire a new habit no matter how much you tell yourself you might want to do that.

My friend asked: "Do you brush your teeth every morning?" and I said "Yes, of course I do!" He suggested that the best way to acquire a new habit was to attach it to an old one, so maybe I should start getting on my knees right before or after I brushed my teeth in the morning.

Actually, I faithfully do a number of things every morning and I found that the best time for me to get on my knees was immediately after I got out of the shower, but before I shaved. And that worked! (There are mornings when I forget to shave – it's the last thing I do before starting the day and I sometimes get distracted near the end of my routine – but I almost never forget to get on my knees.)

What I say on my knees every morning – out loud (another good piece of advice that I received) – has changed regularly and significantly over the past 30 years. I have found this is the only way I can effectively guard against this practice becoming just another boring daily exercise – a routine recitation of the same thing day after day. As I have changed, what I say each morning has also changed. But whatever I say, it is always some variation on "the story I tell myself in the morning about the person I want to be throughout the day". That kind of constant change ensures that it continues to be an "alive and vital" daily practice.

Here's one more example of how this advice has worked for me.

Years ago, I started meditating in the mornings and that practice became a regular habit once I coupled it with finishing my morning cup of coffee.

That was so successful that I decided to add an evening meditation to my practice. But no matter what I did, I just couldn't seem to get the evening "sit" off the ground. Something always seemed to get in the way.

Finally, one night at dinner, I said to my Lady Sara: "You know, I'm always advising people that if they want to form a new habit they should attach it to an old one. And I just haven't been able to develop a regular meditation practice in the evening. But... I do have dinner every night, so from now on I am going to just go downstairs and hit the cushion immediately after we eat at night."

Sara's only comment was: "Well, that sounds like a good idea, but can you wait until I finish cleaning up the kitchen?" She wanted to join me.

And she did... and now she reads something "spiritual" out loud every night after dinner and then we sit in silence together.

It's one of the most intimate things we do every day.

5.

"You can pretend to care, but you can't pretend to be there"

I THINK IT was Sara who first heard this phrase while listening to a motivational tape. Or maybe it was me. We're not sure. We also don't remember who the speaker was on that tape. We both seem to think his name was Bob, but we have no idea what his last name was.

But, whoever you are... thanks, Bob, for this very clarifying and challenging piece of advice!

And it is very much both of those things – clarifying and challenging – because lurking just below the surface of that simple phrase is the unspoken, but unavoidable judgement that – barring special circumstances – if you don't make it *there*, then you obviously don't really *care* all that much.

Sometimes, the moral/ethical questions I face in life can seem so complex and confusing that I'm just not confident about what to do next.

"Do the next right thing!" my friends often suggest and that's a wonderful piece of advice, but it's really not very helpful when I have no clear idea of what the "next right thing" might actually be.

Could you please be a little more specific?

But, in any situations where Bob's maxim *might* apply, it quickly clarifies the issue by assigning "caring" and "being present" to an absolutely equivalent and co-dependent status.

If you care, you show up!

If you don't show up, well... what does that say about how much you really care?

In the end, I have found this to be a reliable litmus test for just how much I *do* care – clearing the muddy waters around what the "next right thing" might be when I am confronted with the "go" or "don't go" decision.

And, over the years I have learned, that when in doubt, the best policy is just to "go" and show up.

One reason this phrase resonated so powerfully with me when I first heard it was that it dovetailed so nicely with something my friend, King, was known to say with some regularity:

> "The most important thing we have to give each other is our physical presence."

The first time he said that to me, we were on our way to a wake of someone we both knew. I was always *very* uncomfortable at wakes, avoiding them whenever possible. In the car, I was justifying that avoidance by complaining to King that "I never know what to say to people!"

"Come on," he said, "there *is* no right thing to say at a wake! That's not what it's about. It's about 'showing up' for the grieving person. It's one of those 'actions speak louder than words' things."

That conversation along with Bob's rather more demanding formulation have influenced a number of good decisions over the years. It does make things pretty simple. Am I going to be the guy who goes? Or am I going to be the guy who fails to show up? (And, how am I going to feel about not showing up when I look at myself in the mirror the next morning?)

I've been to a *lot* of wakes in the past few decades because of this. And, having lived through both of my parent's wakes, I know how important it is for people to actually 'be there' and physically share the profound grief of such a loss.

Sometimes even more is required. Twice in the past decade I've flown from New York to Los Angeles to attend memorial services for men that I knew through business.

Chuck was certainly an important business associate and he was such a well-loved man that my absence would likely never have been noticed by any of the more than 300 people who showed up at the megachurch in Riverside, CA that day. But I went because he was my friend, someone I genuinely cared for and I felt I had to honor that feeling with my presence. If I had taken the easy way out and not gotten on that plane, I would have had significant regrets for some time afterwards.

When Michael, my mentor in the rare book business, died, I arrived in LA around noon, checked into a hotel and then took a cab to the memorial service. The next morning, I caught an early flight back home. Time on the ground in California... something like 19 hours. Worth it? Certainly to me, but perhaps even more so to his lifelong business partner who was devastated by the loss.

And it's not just about the painful duty of going to wakes or memorial services. I have found this advice equally applies to celebrations of all kinds – weddings, christenings, holiday parties, cook outs, Memorial Day parades, etc. – events that I frequently would prefer to dodge if at all possible.

A couple of years ago, Sara and I drove two hours to attend my sister's 80th birthday party. The older I get, the less happy I am about these long drives and of "losing" a beautiful summer day to four hours on the highway. But it was my sister's birthday and it was a big one. And, her daughter – who planned the party – really wanted us to be there for the celebration. Could I have made up some lame excuse of a "prior commitment" for me or for Sara? Of course. But what would that say about my level of caring for my sister and her happiness (not to mention my niece's)?

Let me tell you... I liked looking at *that* guy in the mirror the next morning!

"Caring" is an action word.

6.

"All important decisions must be made on the basis of insufficient data"

Decades ago, I was in a business meeting and we were thrashing around trying to formulate some important elements in the company's strategic plan. Everyone seemed to have their own individual ax to grind and the discussion was growing heated. With no resolution in sight, several people suggested that it would be impossible to move forward until the company paid to have some very expensive in-depth research done.

Arguments then flared up over what this research might cover, how it should be conducted and, most important, whose budget was going to be charged with the expense. The fault lines within the team grew wider and wider.

Finally, the Chief Operating Officer called for silence by saying: "Look... we just don't have the luxury of wasting any more time and money on this. We need to reach some sort of decision *today*! Let me remind you that all important decisions are made on the basis of insufficient data, and we just can't allow ourselves to be paralyzed by the fact that we are missing a few – possibly very important – details at the moment."

The team had definitely wandered far off "into the weeds," arguing over those details rather than focusing on the larger picture – which is the essence of any strategic plan.

Refocused on the broader perspective, everyone was able to stand down a bit, stop defending their own particular piece of turf and in a relatively short time, we were able to agree on a viable plan for how the company should move forward.

After the meeting, I asked our COO where his idea that "all important decisions had to be made on the basis of insufficient data" came from. He told me he had read it in a book by Sheldon Kopp called *If You Meet the Buddha on the Road, Kill Him!*. There is an appendix in that book, he said, entitled "An Eschatological Laundry List" – purporting to present the first 43 items on a much longer list of "Eternal Truths."

The first item on the list is "This is it!?" and it ends with "Learn to forgive yourself, again and again and again and again." The "Eternal Truth" about "all important decisions..." is number 33. (It is a list well worth looking up online and reading... and, yes, that's another piece of useful advice!)

The point is that we should beware the fatal trap of thinking that we must have *all* the facts before making an important decision.

Certainly, it is essential to investigate thoroughly, to gather and weigh as many facts as possible, but holding out for *all* the facts is a fool's errand – especially if that stubborn insistence prevents you from making an important decision about your business (or your life) in a timely fashion.

Learn to live with the fact that you are *never* going to have *all* the facts!

Once again, this advice resonated strongly with me because it fit neatly into something I had been hearing regularly throughout my life.

Ask any one of my brothers: "What was Dad's most memorable expression?" and all three will reply without hesitation: *"Let's do something even if it's wrong!"*

That was my Dad.

He was by nature a man of action and strongly averse to what he called "analysis paralysis."

Dad was diligent and thorough in his research and not prone to rash decisions, but he was *not* a patient man. Sooner or later, he would reach a boiling point and – once his personal dial went into the red zone – the time for investigation and evaluation was over!

Sometimes, it was just his way of ending an interminable discussion over where to go for dinner or which movie to watch. Other times, it was his response to much more serious issues, such as how to handle a difficult situation with a customer or which piece of expensive new equipment the company should buy.

Whatever... it worked for him. That poor Depression-era farm boy with a sixth grade education became a successful and well-respected member of his community, raised a family of six and lived a life he could never have imagined as a young man.

All throughout those years, he had clearly internalized the truth of "all important decisions must be made on the basis of insufficient data" – he just formulated it a little bit differently:

"Let's do something... even if it's wrong!"

When time grows short and decision-time looms... then it's time to judiciously pull the trigger and move on as best you can!

7.

NEVER say: "You shouldn't feel that way!"

And, here we are again, back with my friend, the amazing therapist, Larry.

While Sara and I were in couple's counselling with him, I was once (*just once, Bill?*) upset by something she said and I responded by telling her she had no right to feel that way.

I said it was a *completely* inappropriate reaction.

Larry's response was something to behold!

He interrupted forcefully and told me in no uncertain terms that it was *my* reaction that was "inappropriate" and completely out of line. He said I should *NEVER* criticize Sara by telling her she "shouldn't feel that way."

"People feel the way they feel," he said. "It's their own emotional reality and you can't just blithely dismiss another person's reality like that. It may make no sense to you, but that is, in fact, *the way she feels*. And, people are entitled to their feelings... whatever they may be. Feelings have a primal validity that cannot be denied. They *are* what they *are*! So, please don't ever say anything like that to Sara again!"

I must admit I have struggled with this.

From my own perspective (obviously, so much more accurate!) her response was completely unjustified by the circumstances of the situation, and I was therefore well within my rights to call her out and demand she adopt a more "appropriate" emotional response to the matter.

But over time – I come to so many of these things very slowly – I have realized two things:

> (1) my own argumentative perspective was self-centered and, more important, self-serving in the extreme and

> (2) Larry's observation on human emotions didn't just apply to my Lady Sara, it was equally valid in relation to everyone else I had to deal with in my life.

However reluctantly, I finally had to concede that he was right. Feelings are feelings. They are what they are. And you can never tell anyone "You shouldn't feel that way!" – if that's the way they feel.

For me to "allow" Sara to have her feelings without argument (or, equally important, without me trying to "fix" the way she felt), proved to be one the most important tools Larry ever gave me. His gifts were many, but this one was easily in the top three.

In the beginning, realizing the trouble that resulted whenever I told Sara "you shouldn't feel that way" was enough to convince me that I wanted to make every effort to avoid falling into that particular trap again. It didn't take a tremendous amount of honest recollection and reflection to see that this particular approach had *never* really turned out well.

However, over time, as I studiously refrained from using the forbidden phrase, my silence gradually pushed me in the direction of a completely different response. Rather than judging her reactions by my own, I began trying to understand what it must be like for her to feel that way (and why) – and to react with some empathy.

Unexpectedly, each step away from judgment took me one step closer to compassion. It literally made Sara more interesting to me and this had the blessed effect of increasing the intimacy in our relationship. She became more and more *real* to me – and less a product of my self-centered male delusions.

Increasingly convinced of the rightness of Larry's comments, I have frequently been able to expand this compassionate approach to include friends, relatives and even co-workers. Acknowledging the undeniable reality of other people's feelings and accepting them on their own terms – *really* accepting them for what they are – has had a profound and positive effect on so many of my relationships.

Please don't mistake me. At times, I have found this to be difficult in the extreme.

For instance, one of my best friends has struggled with clinical depression his whole life and I have never been able to understand his worldview or his consistently dark reactions to everyday life. As far as I can see, his circumstance just don't warrant that kind of a response. He's a great guy, bright, witty and engaging, a truly accomplished professional... so he should be happy, right?

In short, he just "shouldn't feel that way!"

But that dark world *is* his Reality. However unjustified from my perspective, his world is not my world and I must accept that. I have no special powers that would magically allow him to see the world from my perspective. All I can do is acknowledge and accept his reality. It is the only way we could ever have continued to be such good friends for the past three decades.

This one change in *my* perspective on other people's perspectives was significant and far-reaching. Other people became more individuated and real and, because of that, I found I could relate to them more readily and more deeply.

Larry's advice has helped me to lay aside my knee-jerk judgments (*at least some of the time*) and whenever I am able to do that, the world invariably becomes wider, broader and far more interesting.

And what's not to like about that?

8.

Pay attention to what you pay attention to

ONE OF THE best books I've read in the past few years was Tim Wu's *The Attention Merchants*. It chronicles the rise of advertising since the 1840s – focusing mainly on its growing presence, influence and impact since the First World War (1914-1918).

Wu awakened me to what a dominant and driving force advertising is in my life and to the fact that I barely register its presence – even as I am literally drowning in it. It's a powerful and ubiquitous part of our economic culture, but I had become almost completely oblivious to this constant bombardment.

Tim's book clearly delineates the history of the ever-increasing ways that advertisers have invaded our lives, stolen our attention and then converted it into cash. Who knew it wasn't always this way?

One of the things I really appreciated about his book was the fact that Wu opened and closed it with a nod to William James, the great American psychologist and philosopher. On page 7, he notes: "As William James observed, we must reflect that, when we reach the end of our days, our life experience will equal what we have paid attention to, whether by choice or default."

I must say that knocked me out the first time I read it. So much so that I began reading James' 1890 masterwork, *The Principles of Psychology*, in which he devotes an entire chapter to "Attention." The opening section of that chapter makes this important observation:

> Millions of items of the outward order are present to my senses which never properly enter into my experience. Why? Because they have no *interest* for me. *My experience is what I agree to attend to.* Only those items which I *notice* shape my mind – without selective interest, experience is an utter chaos. Interest alone gives accent and emphasis, light and shade, background and foreground – intelligible perspective, in a word. It varies in every creature...

Wu returned to James in the final paragraph of his book, reiterating that "it was William James... [who] held that our life experience would ultimately amount to whatever we had paid attention to" before offering these concluding words:

> If we desire a future that avoids the enslavement of the propaganda state as well as the narcosis of the consumer and celebrity culture, we must first acknowledge the preciousness of our attention

and resolve not to part with it as cheaply or unthinkingly as we so often have. And then we must act, individually and collectively, to make our attention our own again, and so reclaim ownership of the very experience of living.

The Attention Merchants very effectively rubbed my nose in how inattentive I was to the prevalence and the evils of advertising, but James' comment that "our life experience would ultimately amount to whatever we had paid attention to" was even more powerful. I resolved to pay more attention to what I paid attention to – something I would not have done without the advice of these two intelligent and profoundly insightful men.

When I first read William James' words, I was reminded of something that happened a few years ago. After standing on our back deck admiring Sara's large and beautiful garden, I wandered inside and told her how gorgeous it looked and how much I appreciated all the hard work she put into it. "Did you like that new pink flowering shrub I just planted on the border?" she asked. "No," I had to admit, "I didn't notice it."

Sara was shocked at my lack of attention to the details and, in my own defense, I tried to point out that, standing on the deck, I was more of a "big picture guy." I was taking in the *whole* garden, I told her, and not really paying much attention to individual plants. She was even more appalled.

I thought it would amuse my artist-friend, Kevin when I told him that story a few weeks later. He did laugh, but not for the reasons I expected. "That's funny," he said, "because when I look at Sara's garden what I see is color, light and shadow."

So here we have three people's completely different *experiences* of our backyard garden because they pay attention to completely different things.

Even more striking was something that happened a couple of summers ago on a trip back from Maine. Sara was driving and we were about half way home when she said "Look, there's another hawk. It's the third one I've seen since we left the house." Now Sara is *always* seeing wildlife while driving – most especially hawks – but I rarely (if ever) see any. How could I be so completely oblivious to something as beautiful and majestic as a hawk? I had missed three of them in the past two hours? Yes!

I must say, I found that kind of surprising myself. *So... what was it I was looking at while she was noticing all these hawks?* I spent the next 30 minutes paying attention to what I was paying attention to as we rode in the car and discovered that what I paid attention to during that half hour (and throughout most of my life, I later realized) was *WORDS*. I was busy reading every single word in sight – exit sign words, building-sign words, license plate words, car make and model words, advertising sign words. Words, words, words!

Noticing this didn't mean that I suddenly stopped doing it. In fact, constantly reading words seems to be pretty deeply ingrained into who I am and how I operate. *I'm a word guy!*

But I *have* been able to do something about it. Now when we go out in the car, I typically make a concerted effort to pay attention to something other than words. Sometimes it's the stone walls (lots of those in Connecticut!), sometimes it's the trees, or just the bark on trees, sometimes it's the unsightliness of the telephone and power wires (which are such a blight on our landscape), sometimes it's the clouds and the changing colors of the sky. But whatever I'm paying attention to these days on our drives, I am making a conscious effort to ensure that I'm not just looking for words.

To once more quote James' *Principles of Psychology*: "each of us literally chooses, by his way of attending to things, what sort of universe he shall appear to himself to inhabit."

Wow! Challenging advice, but, it has definitely helped make my life just a little bit richer and more interesting by consciously redirecting my attention to things that I have not typically noticed before.

9.

Embrace the fact that we are all different

THIS PIECE OF advice gradually grew out of my own experience and I have struggled mightily over the years to wrap my head – and my everyday perspective – around it! It's been a long, slow process of realization and an even longer battle to internalize it.

For decades, my simple solution to "the mystery of other people's minds" was to presume *they all thought exactly the same way I did.*

And, if they didn't, well... they certainly should!

As simple as that.

I was blindly unaware of this "it's all about what I think" perspective – at least in those stark and naked terms – but it was certainly how I operated. *I believed it!*

The result was that on more than one occasion I found myself loudly declaring: "Well.. that's all wrong! Let me tell you how you *should* be thinking about this!"

My unconscious belief about the "sameness of our thoughts" was the result of a number of different influences – several from my upbringing – but I believe that many more can be traced back to a number of foundational elements in our Western culture.

Take, for instance, the classic philosophical proof "All men are mortal / Socrates is a man / Therefore, Socrates is mortal" or the famous American political statement that "All men are created equal." *(There are enough examples of this kind of thing to easily fill this page!)*

Unconsciously internalizing these familiar quotes (along with so many other similar cultural signals), I had blindly fallen into the trap of believing that "All men are the SAME."

Nothing could be further from the truth.

My painfully slow awakening to the reality of these fundamental differences between people began in earnest during the early days of my relationship with the Lady Sara. The more intimate we became and the more I learned about how she thought, the more impossible it became to ignore how very different that was from the way that I thought.

In fact, it was *nothing* like the way I thought!

All too frequently, we seemed to be talking about different things or, at least, coming at them from such completely different perspectives that they might as well have been different things.

Over time, the first blush of this insight grew until I had to admit that it was not just Sara who was substantially different from me. *Everyone* – regardless of their age, sex, wealth, class, upbringing or cultural conditioning – experienced the world and processed those experiences in ways that were far different from mine.

I have, for instance, several friends that I frequently have trouble "following" when we talk. It seems as if they are almost "playing with a different deck of cards". Whatever premises and foundational materials they are working with are so different from my own thought patterns that I frequently have a hard time just "getting" them, no matter how diligently I might try to understand exactly what it is they are trying to tell me.

That doesn't mean the situation is hopeless. But until I recognized, acknowledged and accommodated the fundamental differences in other people's experience, their processing and thinking, the problem *was* insurmountable.

Once I realized the necessity of accommodating other people's mindsets, and committed to being attentive rather than just presumptive and judgmental, *real* conversations with *real* communication all of a sudden started to become possible.

I have, to give just one example, a good friend who is very religious. My own worldview, on the other hand, includes no supernatural elements whatsoever. This doesn't mean that my friend is *wrong*. He just experiences and processes the world differently from me. We may both be contemporary American males with many common, foundational experiences, but we have also been exposed to and lived *completely different spiritual lives* and those experiences have resulted in two very different ways of "being" in the world.

Still, once we both acknowledged that fact and then respectfully honored our differences, we found that we can have truly meaningful – even deeply spiritual – conversations about our respective (and sometimes complimentary) opinions of the things that matter most to us in life.

Who would have thought such a thing possible?

We *are* all different. It is a basic fact of life. Becoming fully aware of that fact and then acting on it has opened up new perspectives in all my relationships and thereby enriched my life immeasurably.

Think of it as the most extreme form of *democratic pluralism* imaginable.

10.

"I can really identify with that emotional cowardice..."

MY FRIEND JACK was a retired police detective and one of the most spiritually courageous people I have ever known. He was justly revered as the closest thing we had to a "wise man" in my circle of friends.

Who would have thought that such a street-hardened guy could ever rise to such levels of compassion and wisdom? It would have been much more likely, after his many years on the streets of the inner city, if Jack had become a cynic of the first order. But he came away from "the job" with an amazing ability to see the human side of almost every situation. This was balanced by the fact that he was equally famous for candidly speaking his mind and offering advice – often when none was being asked for.

I was in my office one day and Jack and I were on the phone talking about an upcoming social event when one of our employees walked by my open door. He was the supervisor for half of the company's workers and I was extremely unhappy with the way he was doing his job.

I offhandedly mentioned this to Jack, confessing that, each morning as I drove to work, I felt like there was a rock in the pit of my stomach because I knew I was going to have to face this situation sooner or later. But, I noted, every day something seemed to come up that prevented me from confronting this employee with how unhappy I was with his performance.

When I reached the end of this unplanned confessional, Jack casually said, "I can really identify with that emotional cowardice", and then went on to relate a couple of personal stories where he repeatedly avoided emotionally uncomfortable situations – and then noted the disproportionate price he had to pay for each of those incidents in the long run.

I was more than a little taken aback.

Is this guy calling me a coward!!?

Well, yes... he was.

He was pointing out that I was certainly *acting* like an "emotional" coward and, once I got over my shock, I could hardly deny the truth of it. Here I was, not addressing an ongoing and personally upsetting situation for fear of my own emotional reactions and to avoid the inevitable emotional fallout between this employee and myself. I have always hated confrontation and avoided it whenever possible, but I had comfortably packaged that kind of behavior as the virtue of acceptance rather than a failure of courage on my part.

While I can recognize, acknowledge and own many of my faults, self-identifying as a coward was something that I just could not do. *Anything but that!*

The very next day I had a sit-down with that employee (which I have already related in Chapter 3) because I knew that any further delay would be unavoidable proof-positive of my emotional cowardice.

Enough cannot be said for those rare friends who have the courage to tell you the truth as they see it, when they see it.

Jack was that kind of friend.

As I thought about this, I began to notice more and more situations where I wasn't doing something or I wasn't saying something because of my emotional cowardice – and that awareness forced me to change my behavior and act with a bit more courage on several of those occasions.

One place where this came up with some regularity was in relation to those difficult conversations with my wife, the Lady Sara. I have been known to say on more than just a few occasions that the five most courageous things I've done in the past couple of decades have all started with the words: "Sara, there's something I think we need to talk about…"

Summoning up the courage to begin one of "those" conversations, was surely helped by the training we got from our therapist, Larry, on the necessity of having "the conversation before the conversation" (see Chapter #26). Nonetheless, initiating one of those conversations – which can so swiftly and easily wander off into an emotional minefield – always called for a significant amount of emotional courage on my part.

One other incident comes to mind that Jack's advice helped me with tremendously. This was during my pre-Sara, single days. We had a gorgeous, intelligent and witty client and I was dying to ask her out on a date. But she was so gorgeous, so intelligent and so witty that I couldn't bring myself to pick up the phone and call her.

My self-justification for this failure was my long-held belief that I was just a painfully shy guy. This was a great story to be telling myself, but sometime after that seminal conversation with Jack, I realized, to my horror, that I wasn't "shy"... I was just terrified of rejection!

So, again, the self-talk turned to: "So here's another place where you are a coward? Is that it, Schaberg?"

Again, I found it impossible to live with myself once I realized my bogus story about being "shy" was nothing more than a carefully crafted cover for my emotional cowardice.

I called – I really had no choice once I had put it to myself that way – and she declined my invitation to dinner.

And... I *didn't* die of the rejection (as I had been so certain I would)!

But, at least, I wasn't going to die a coward either.

11.

"There are only five things worth fighting about in a marriage"

I HAVE ALREADY said that the first "rule" we try to live by in our house is "Loving someone means *acting* as if their happiness is important to you." "The Five Things" is our second "rule" and it can be a lifesaver when the way forward according to "rule" #1 is not as clear as I would like it to be.

One Monday, several years ago, I was on the phone with my friend Steve and he was recounting what sounded like some really unacceptable things his wife had said and done the previous weekend. As the story got more and more troubling, I was preparing my spiel of sympathy along with a large dose of advice for what I thought he should be doing in this dreadful situation.

But Steve stopped me dead in my tracks when – at the end of his story – he said: "But, I have decided there are only five things worth fighting about in a marriage and so I let the whole thing slide and it just blew over."

Now, my friend Steve is a really smart guy, someone whose opinion I truly value, but this statement was so bizarre that I just had to challenge him.

"There are only five things worth fighting about in a marriage?" I asked skeptically. "Really?... Well, if that's true," I said (grabbing for pen and paper), "then I need to know what those five things are!"

"No, no, that's not what I'm talking about... you don't understand," he said. "It's not like there are just five and only five definite things worth fighting about in any marriage. It's just that I've made a decision to adopt the belief that there are only five things worth fighting about in *my* marriage, and whenever something comes up between us, I ask myself: "*Is this one of the five things?*" And, it almost never is. So, I just let it go and don't fight with her about whatever it is.'"

One defense Steve offered for this crazy-sounding advice was to note how regularly they had fought in the past, and how he could barely remember the cause of those fights a month later.

"If the cause is really so forgettable," he said, "why would I ever want to go there in the first place? The 'five things' rule provides me with the pause I need to consider the cause for a moment and then – almost always – sidestep the battle."

I was completely floored by this strange and very counter-intuitive solution to frequent family fights and that night I brought it home to my Lady Sara. However ridiculous it might sound at first, I was intrigued. We talked about it off-and-on for several days – considering it from several angles – and finally decided to try it as a possible solution for some of the "speed bumps" in our own relationship.

And it has worked amazingly well. Over and over again. "The Five Things" is a powerful yardstick that allows me – as Steve predicted – to hit the "pause button" before reacting in a way that I would likely later regret.

My classic story for explaining how "The Five Things" actually works involves a redbud tree.

We had bought a piece of land that adjoined our lot with the neighbors who lived on the other side – and then split it equally between us. There was a redbud tree near the front of that property and Sara disliked it and wanted to cut it down. I really liked the tree. Both of our neighbors on the other side really liked the tree.

One day, my friend Mike the landscaper asked: "So, what should I be doing about that redbud tree out front?" When I told him about the three favorable opinions and Sara's negative reaction to the tree, Mike replied: "So, you *don't* want me to cut it down, right?"

"Wrong," I said. "The tree is on our side of the dividing line so the neighbor's opinion doesn't really count. And, as far as I'm concerned, although I really do like that tree, it's not one of the five things, so go ahead and cut it down."

Definitely *NOT* one of the five things.

Here's another story about how this works from the other side.

Having become somewhat notorious among my friends as "The Five Things Guy," one of them approached me and told me about how his very formidable new wife had gotten between him and his 20-year-old daughter from a former marriage – effectively driving his daughter away from him.

"But," he said, "it's not one of the five things, so I'm not going to make an issue of it or argue with her about it."

I told him I thought that was a terrible conclusion and that, it seemed to me, his decision was based more on his abject fear (terror!) of arguing with his current wife than anything else. His ongoing relationship with his daughter was, in my opinion, most certainly one of the five things that was worth fighting about in his marriage.

It's a hard concept for a lot of people to wrap their heads around. Even after I have given a full explanation of how this works for Sara and me, friends frequently come back to the place where we started and wonder sadly: "So, there aren't any five definite things?"

No there aren't. *There are no carved-in-stone five things!*

It's all situational. A moving target to be decided in the moment.

But if you decide, like my friend Steve, that there *ARE* only five things worth fighting about in your marriage, it can be one of the most useful tools imaginable in navigating the sometimes-treacherous waters of interpersonal relationships.

Try it!

If your experience is anything like ours, you will be happily surprised at how well it works.

12.

"Identify the places where you encounter the spiritual and go there often"

THIS IS ANOTHER piece of advice I heard while listening to an "inspirational" cassette tape several years ago. I don't remember the exact topic or the speaker's name, but he was offering suggestions on how to enlarge your spiritual life – a project I have devoted some time and attention to (with irregular effort!) over the years.

Throughout his talk, the speaker leaned more heavily on the "God" part than I cared for – reliance on a Supreme Being is not my favored path to spiritual growth – but he caught my attention profoundly when he suggested one simple non-denominational tool for growing spiritually.

"Identify the places where you encounter God and go there often," he said.

His strong emphasis on a Deity didn't resonate with my own belief system, but I immediately realized that substituting the word "spiritual" for "God" would certainly work for me.

(Of course, if that original phrasing works for you, *by all means go for it!*)

My slight reformulation of this piece of advice became something of a personal mantra and it was extremely helpful as I explored new paths on my own spiritual journey. How could it not? There is no dogma whatsoever in relying on my personal encounters with spirituality. The suggestion is open-ended, experimental, experiential and pluralistic in the extreme.

I was raised a devout Roman Catholic and have never attended a public school in my life. After high school, I spent two years studying for the priesthood before getting into a heated doctrinal dispute with the Church and left the seminary. During the next two years, I gradually discarded Catholicism, then Christianity, then Deism, then Monotheism, then Agnosticism and finally Theism itself.

I am a firm believer in "the spiritual element of life" but I was hard pressed to explain exactly what I meant by that phrase when people asked for a clarification – which happened with some regularity because I like to talk about "spiritual" topics.

For me, the remarkable power of this advice was that I didn't have to find the words or the arguments for what I meant by "the spiritual element in my life." I simply had to pay attention and *IDENTIFY* the *PLACES* where I *FELT* that I was having an *EXPERIENCE* that might justifiably – under an undefined, but very broad umbrella

– be described as *SPIRITUAL*... and then *GO THERE* as often as possible.

In practical, day-to-day terms, this meant I had to "turn on my radar" and then keep it up as I "swept" my world for anything that might feel remotely spiritual to me.

That proved to be a far more fruitful and far less frustrating than trying to formulate a concrete 'sound bite' for what I meant by "my spiritual life."

And, once I started doing this, I got spiritual radar "blips" in some very interesting places.

Several of these were pretty obvious. I have been in the practice of getting on my knees every morning and reciting an ever-changing laundry list of affirmations for years. I thought of this as a daily exercise of telling myself a story – out loud – about the kind of person I wanted to be that day. Spiritual, for sure!

Talking with my wife and really listening to what she was saying was, I realized, a spiritual exercise. The same was true of sharing with friends and being truly attentive to what they were saying (rather than formulating what I was going to say once they stopped talking). VERY spiritual!

My beautiful Maine Coon cat, Mischa, offered daily opportunities to get out of my head and pay close attention to a completely different and much beloved lifeform. Definitely spiritual!

Splashing along the water's edge at our nearby beach while making a conscious effort to "be there" with the four ancient elements (earth, water, air and fire [the sun]), experiencing the look and feel and sound of the waves – rather than being off somewhere in my head – is a profoundly spiritual exercise.

Sitting and meditating every morning by myself, and every night with my Lady Sara are surely spiritual opportunities for me.

And each of these sits is always preceded by some short, ever changing readings from "spiritual" books. (A couple of years ago I discovered Mary Oliver's poems and if reading one of those every morning doesn't qualify as a spiritual exercise, then I don't know what in the world does!)

Honestly thinking about and trying to confront my own mortality is *always* a deeply spiritual exercise.

Perhaps my favorite and personally weird "identify the places" story happened late one night as I was driving home from JFK airport – playing the *Layla* album at top volume. Halfway through the song, "Key to the Highway" (which I had listened to at least 2,000 times!), I realized that I was physically and mentally overwhelmed with JOY, and I had to admit that whatever else it might be, this was surely a spiritual experience.

What do all of those experiences have in common?

I'm not sure.

But if there *is* a common thread in all the different times I've felt that I was "having an encounter with the spiritual", the unifying element seems to be – to one degree or another – that I have been "outside myself", present and "a part of" rather than "absent and caught in my self-centered dreams" (to freely quote one of my favorite Buddhist teachers, Charlotte Joko Beck).

So... what might show up on *YOUR* radar if you tuned it to the "places where your encounter the spiritual" channel?

13.

"Whatever truth there is exists in the experience, not in the explanation"

In 2018, my friend, Jay – who is the program director for a Daoist center in Sedona – invited me and thirty-four other people to Arizona for a weekend retreat.

To one degree or another, we were all friends of Jay's, but that was perhaps all we had in common. In fact, we were a widely divergent group – most especially if you sorted us out by our religious beliefs. The group included fundamentalist Christians, devout Catholics, committed Protestants, Buddhists, Daoists, Deists, agnostics and atheists.

It was a really diverse and interesting crowd!

Jay had invited us there *because* of our differences and also because of the common thread that he saw running through each of our lives. We were all committed to living "spiritual" lives, whatever that might mean in the context of our own understandings.

His hope was that we might spend a weekend organized around a program of open dialogue, allowing each of us to see around the corners of our dogmatic differences, and hopefully find the path for some candid communication about whatever *common elements* we might be able to discover within our very different approach to living a "spiritual life".

Friday night and all day Saturday, we would sit in a big circle together before splitting off into a number of ever-changing six-person breakout groups – each time with a different topic assigned for discussion (meditation, spiritual habits or rituals, prayer, spiritual growth, favorite books, core beliefs, etc.).

In the beginning, some of these sessions were understandably a bit contentious, but as the weekend progressed, we all became much less defensive about our own entrenched positions and began to genuinely listen to one another.

It really was an amazing thing to be a part of!

Late Sunday morning, after two final breakout sessions, we sat in the big circle for the last time and everyone got a chance to talk about what the weekend had been like for them. While the wide difference of our beliefs was still evident, there was also a new and very real tolerance exhibited by all of the attendees towards the spiritual paths that others were walking.

A feeling of collegial respect dominated the circle.

We had genuinely seen and heard each other.

During that final session, my favorite comment came from Joe – a committed atheist – who shared what had most impressed him over the past two days. He said he noticed that when we confined our talk to our individual *experiences* of the spiritual, he could understand, appreciate and sometimes even identify with those experiences. It seemed to him that it was only when we went off into our *explanations* of those experiences that the contentious dogmatic differences and their seemingly insurmountable difficulties arose. "Let's face it," he said, "you can't argue with someone's *experience!*"

I was profoundly impressed by that comment. It certainly resonated with me as I reflected on the conversations I had participated in over the previous two days.

I didn't want to lose sight of that powerful observation and a couple of weeks later – with Joe's permission – I reduced it to the phrase "Whatever truth there is exists in the experience, not in the explanation."

That was my most important 'take away' from my weekend with those 35 people in Sedona.

Whenever I remember it, Joe's comment reminds me of how I habitually spend almost all my time in my head, formulating reasons and explanations – while hurrying right past the raw data of the experiences that triggered those constantly streaming thoughts.

The tendency to immediately begin formulating explanations for everything we encounter in life is surely one of the things that makes us human. But to do so without paying any real attention to the physical, mental, emotional or spiritual events that prompted those thoughts in the first place is for me to deny a *very* large part of my reality.

There is so much more to life than just thinking!

And, beyond the need to pay more attention to my own foundational experiences, I also have to constantly remind myself that whatever explanations I *do* come up with relative to my experiences are not necessarily the same as the ones *you* might come up with from very similar experiences of your own.

Or, as Joe said to me in a later conversation along these same lines: "Yes... the problem with the Truth is that there are so many versions of it."

So many very different experiences followed by even more *different* explanations...

Amen!

14.

"First, climb out of the cauldron..."

SARA AND I sit with a small Zen group on Thursday evenings and this very helpful piece of advice came to me from our Buddhist teacher, Jane.

We had been close friends with a married couple for over thirty years before they divorced. We continued to see them both socially for several months, but gradually, the wife grew more and more distant until she had completely removed herself from our wide circle of friends.

Soon afterwards, we began to hear some vicious stories she was spreading about us and, most hurtfully, about my Lady Sara.

I had no intention of actively engaging with these attacks, but the more I heard of them, the more upset I became. It got so bad that my two daily meditations were pretty much overwhelmed with anger, resentment and arguments in my head. I was furious, constantly rehearsing all the things I was going to say to this woman should the opportunity present itself.

Thankfully, the opportunity never did present itself, but the anger and the mental arguments just went on and on.

After several weeks of this, I finally confided the situation to Jane during one of our private talks, telling her about the terrible time I was having letting go of this anger and of these constant negative conversations in my head.

Jane listened patiently and then said: "You need to realize that this woman is obviously in a lot of pain. Try visualizing her being trapped in a giant cauldron of boiling water. Then realize that your problem is that *you are in the cauldron with her!*"

At this point, she had my full attention. Both of those images resonated strongly.

Then, Jane said: "The first thing you need to do is to climb out of the cauldron. Imagine yourself doing that and walking away 20 paces. Then, turn around and see just how much pain that poor woman is in... and try to have some compassion for her."

Brilliant. Just brilliant!

Sara was suffering along similar lines and we discussed this wise advice all the way home that night in the car.

I would love to say that Jane's advice allowed me to instantly turn the corner on my problem, but that was not the case.

Resentment, anger, and those imaginary conversations continued to crop up with regularity, but every time I caught myself moving into that negative space, I would visualize the cauldron and then imagine climbing out, walking away, turning around and try to project some compassion back towards my suffering friend.

Gradually, this began to work for me. Every time I performed this exercise, I was able to generate just a little bit more compassion. The result was that, over time, these angry flare ups became less and less frequent and then, eventually, stopped altogether.

So, Jane's advice wasn't an instant solution, but it did work – just as long as I put in the time and effort to work it.

Sara's experience was similar.

It's also interesting to note how shared experiences like this can facilitate better communication in a marriage. Over the past couple of years, this image of the cauldron has become something of a cliché in our house; a wonderful bit of shorthand to describe the kind of emotional turmoil that we all find ourselves in from time to time.

These days, if I tell Sara that "I'm really in the cauldron with...," she immediately knows what I am talking about and, more important, she then knows exactly how to be helpful... by encouraging me to "walk away" and try to be compassionate.

On the other hand, we have given each other permission to gently say "So... you're in the cauldron with that one, huh?" as a way of pointing out the reality of the situation. (Sometimes it's hard to know – on your own – that you are in the cauldron... even as the water boils furiously all around you.)

Thanks, Jane! It was a VERY helpful piece of advice.

So... who (or what) might you be in the cauldron with these days?

15.

"What we need here is complete transparency!"

SARA AND I had been together a little over two years when we had a huge argument that almost ended our relationship. Fortunately, our outstanding therapist, Larry, gave us some sage advice which allowed us to survive as a couple.

The problem was this. One of my former lovers, Evelyn, would drop by my office every so often – conveniently arriving right around lunchtime. While I am passionately committed to monogamy, I was never reluctant to spend some time in public with this very pretty woman. Nor did it hurt that Evelyn was just naturally flirtatious, which always provided a nice boost for my ego!

However, I never told Sara about any of these unscheduled lunches. Although she is not a particularly jealous woman, Sara most definitely saw Evelyn as a potential threat to our relationship. But from my perspective, I *knew* I wasn't doing anything overtly wrong at these lunches, so why *needlessly* upset Sara by telling her that Evelyn had made another one of her unscheduled visits, and I had taken her to lunch?

My final lunch with Evelyn was on a Friday, and the following Monday I learned that she had been brutally murdered over the weekend. At lunch, she had told me stories about her new boyfriend and I suspected some of that information might be of interest to the police. I phoned and shared what I knew with them. When I got home that night, I told Sara about our lunch, about what had happened to Evelyn, and about my call to the police.

Sara was devastated.

The story I was telling myself was that there was absolutely nothing wrong with what I had been doing, and I felt I was just protecting Sara from unnecessary and unjustified upset by not telling her about these "innocent" meetings. But, from *her* perspective, my "secretly" seeing Evelyn was an unforgivable lie of omission – one that completely destroyed her trust in me.

Over the next few weeks, we spent many painful hours alone, together and in therapy as I continued to defend myself, while she insisted she had lost faith in me and that our relationship was all but over. Our therapist, always the champion of better communication, pointed out that this was not a case of poor communication or even miscommunication, but rather something completely different. It was a blatantly *willful lack* of communication on my part.

To counter the "logic" of my defense, Larry methodically whittled away at my reasons for believing that is was somehow my job to "protect" Sara from being upset (and to unilaterally decide when it was appropriate to do that).

He went on to say that we could only be in a truly intimate relationship if we habitually shared *everything* about ourselves with each other.

"What you two need to adopt," he said, "is a policy and a practice of complete transparency."

Evelyn's murder was never solved, but her death did cause a radical change in our relationship once I honestly embraced this idea of unfiltered openness with each other.

At first, I was extremely reluctant to adopt this proposal. It was scary. I was sure it would lead to more – rather than fewer – arguments.

Wasn't this practice of absolute truth-telling going to be the *cause* of some really big problems rather than any kind of *solution*?

I just didn't see how this could actually work out for us in "the real world."

But with Larry's encouragement and Sara's wholehearted support, I finally agreed that, going forward, I would stop deciding what I should and should not be telling her. I would tell her EVERYTHING.

And while I can't say this has always been an easy road to follow, it is far, far better than the old path which led directly to our occasional fights and to the inevitable loss of faith once previously undisclosed behavior was revealed.

Today, Sara knows everything going on in my life, my head and my heart.

EVERYTHING!

And, perhaps most important, knowing that I am going to faithfully report back to my wife whatever is going on in my life, my head and my heart has proven to be an amazingly powerful moral compass for me.

If I am tempted to do something which sounds like a good idea to me, but the thought of telling Sara about it afterwards feels problematic, then it is clearly not something I should be doing.

As my friend Jack (he of the "I really identify with that emotional cowardice" line) was known to say with some regularity: "there is no right way to do the wrong thing".

And "secret" lunches with former lovers are always the wrong thing to be doing... however 'innocent' I might believe them to be!

If it's got to be "secret"... there is always a problem with the action.

16.

"Compassion can never co-exist with judgement"

A FEW MONTHS after I started a regular meditation practice, I discovered that my friend, Ray, had also just begun to sit daily. At the time, he was the only local person I knew who was doing anything like this, so we began getting together to share our experiences with meditation.

The Buddhist teacher that Ray was formally sitting with once a month was also a Roman Catholic priest. I found this a bit odd at first, but Ray is a staunch Roman Catholic and the arrangement seemed to make sense to both of them – however contradictory and confusing it might seem to me.

One thing we did with some regularity was to recommend helpful books to each other. One day, Ray called to say he had just ordered me a copy of *The Way of the Heart* and he was really excited to know what I thought about it. I was more than a little skeptical when the book arrived.

It was written by Henri Nouwen, a renowned Protestant teacher of pastoral theology, and the subtitle read: *Connecting with God Through Prayer, Wisdom, and Silence*. It certainly wasn't anything I would have picked up on my own and, I must admit, I was more than a little reluctant to start reading it. But, despite the fact that Ray hadn't finished reading the book himself, he was already checking to see what I thought of the first chapter.

The Way of the Heart has three major sections (Solitude, Silence & Prayer) and I had barely begun the "Solitude" section before I put the book down. It was way too Christian and, worse yet, far too "Calvinist" for my tastes.

The next time he asked, I told Ray I had stopped reading… "it just isn't my kind of book," I said.

Having recently finished the book himself, Ray was disappointed. He said if I would only give it a chance and put in the time – "it is, after all, less than a hundred pages long!" – he was sure I would find it rewarding.

Although my previous experience with the book was not encouraging, I was reluctant to refuse this request. After all, Ray had read more than one book that I had recommended to him. It was clearly time for me to set aside my resistance and return the favor.

While I did continue to bristle at the book's overt Christian religiosity – souls, sin, redemption, demons, temptation, "the abyss of iniquity," "our journey to our eternal home," etc. – I did stumble across exactly what Ray had promised. After using the word "compassion" nine times in two pages, Nouwen drilled his point home by saying: "Compassion can never co-exist with judgement."

That stopped me dead in my tracks. I underlined it, highlighted it, put a big star out in the margin and dogeared the page. That sentence alone was enough justification for me to be reading this book.

This one has been a *huge* struggle for me. It is certainly one of the most challenging pieces of advice I have ever received. Being judgmental is admittedly a universal human trait, but I have always – in the very deepest recess of my heart – considered it to be one of my most outstanding skill sets.

Who better than me – the intelligent, educated, sophisticated, Discerning One – to decide what's right and wrong, who's acting well or speaking badly? Who is more qualified to render the decisive opinion on the worthiness of a proposal... or a song... or even that picture hanging on the wall?

Just ask me. I'm your guy!

And, even if you're not asking, I have this constant stream of chatter going through my head where I perpetually evaluate everyone and everything around me – all too frequently unfavorably.

The moral high ground is so seductive and enticing!

My old therapist would ask me with some regularity when one or more of my problematic behaviors came up: "So what's in it for you? You wouldn't keep doing that if you weren't getting something out of it!"

If you're asking about my judgmentalism, I know the answer to that question and I'm ashamed to admit it: being judgmental lets me feel superior. It makes me feel powerful and omniscient. It's the place where I am always in the right, where I am the final arbiter of all things human and divine!

Understanding and admitting that crass motivation is embarrassing in the extreme and still I catch myself very righteously enjoying that high moral ground on regular occasions.

Worse yet, there is a price to be paid for being so blithely judgmental. A big price. The complete sentence in Nouwen's book reads: "Compassion can never co-exist with judgment because judgment creates the distance, the distinction, which prevents us from really being with the other."

Judgment is isolating.

Compassion is inclusive.

The choice is mine. One or the other. I can't have them both at the same time.

Damn!

For me, this "compassion versus judgement" is literally a daily challenge – when I can remember it, pay attention to it and then actually catch myself in the act. But, to be honest, for all my supposed attention and efforts, compassion doesn't come into the picture anywhere near as often as it could or should.

The Buddha would call such behavior 'unskillful'.

I call it profoundly embarrassing.

17.

"So... what has become clear to you since the last time we met?"

I STOLE THIS amazingly useful phrase from Ralph Waldo Emerson (1803-1882), the great American Transcendentalist philosopher.

In an age without radio, television, recorded music or the internet, social dinners in Emerson's time were typically followed by musical performances and/or card games. But the most highly prized element of those gatherings – the thing that made an evening truly memorable and worth attending – was the lively and enlivening conversation between the guests.

It was an age in which conversation was considered to be an art form.

Emerson was famous for deflecting the dull and boring topics that could so easily dominate these evenings by directing the talk in a more intellectual direction. He did so by choosing a likely partner and then asking him (or, on occasion, her – we must not forget that Margaret Fuller was often in attendance): "So... what has become clear to you since the last time we met?"

Emerson's ploy was almost certain to turn a typically mundane dinner party into something more closely resembling a proper salon; one where people engaged in meaningful conversation, exchanging ideas and opinions as they considered and discussed what had recently changed in their intellectual, emotional, philosophical, spiritual or religious landscape.

No more boring talk! On to more interesting ideas and substantive thoughts!

You go, Emerson!

I have found this to be a powerful conversational gambit when I've used it myself. It immediately eliminates children, spouses, relatives, friends, politics, sports and the weather as an acceptable answer – demanding, instead, a genuine first-person response of one sort or another.

Bringing up this question with seldom-seen friends has proven to be regularly enlightening. So many different reactions and responses! So many varied windows and pathways into the lives of others. So quickly can we go from shallow to deep.

(Of course, I never propose a conversation like this without having at least some idea of what my own contribution might be. On several occasions, the "Emerson Question" has prompted me to share one of the thirty things that I have been writing about here.)

By their very nature, the conversations that follow this question almost always include a high degree of honesty along with a fair amount of vulnerability – which invariably results in greater intimacy.

And so... the friendships deepen.

Over the years, my most frequent partner in these conversations has been my friend, David – one of the finest, most thoughtful and most engaging men I have ever met. David is a true "kindred spirit," but he has, unfortunately, lived on the other side of the continent for the past twenty-five years.

Although we try to stay in touch regularly by phone, there is just too much to talk about. An hour can fly by very quickly, leaving a number of important topics unfinished or completely untouched.

But, when we do happen to be on the same side of the country at the same time, David and I always block out a full morning or afternoon so that we can get completely caught up.

And – after the always obligatory update on wives, children, grandchildren and our respective businesses – one or the other of us will inevitably bring up the "Emerson Question".

Then the *real* conversation begins!

It has been the most important thing we have done over the past twenty-five years to keep our friendship alive and vibrant.

18.

Where would a person have to be standing to see things that way?

BACK HOME AFTER my California friend, Jay, had *finally* convinced me of the benefits of meditation – something he had been trying to do for more than five years – I floundered badly in my first attempts to start a regular practice. At the time, I didn't know a single person in Connecticut who meditated daily, which meant there was no one I could turn to locally for help on how to go about actually *doing* this strange new thing.

Clearly... I needed a book!

So, I called Jay and he recommended that I start with Eckhart Tolle's *The Power of Now*.

That book proved to be a real challenge. Within the first few pages, I found myself rejecting one statement after another.

What is Tolle *talking* about when he says things like it's all about learning "how to free yourself from enslavement to the mind."

"Enslavement to the mind!" What do you think I'm reading this book with!

Or... "You believe you *are* your mind. This is a delusion."

Really! How can this intimately 'felt' identity of "me" with my own mind possibly be a delusion?

My first 'breakthrough' came when I hit page 22 and read that "To the ego, the present moment hardly exists. Only past and future are considered important... observe your mind and you'll see that this is how it works."

My first reaction to this was a fairly loud guffaw. I was a guy who was very much "of the moment". Wasn't I *obviously* living my life in the present! Where else could I be doing that?

I set out to disprove this ridiculous claim and several times a day over the next week, I would stop to see exactly where my mind was at that very moment.

Uh, oh... I was appalled to discover it was *never* in the present. It was *always* in the past or the future. The man was right!

Who knew?

Not me... I was 63 years old and shocked to learn something so profound, so basic, so true *and* so revolutionary about myself. This was obviously *extremely important* information about 'me' that I had been unaware of for my entire life.

That simple experiment – grounded in my own personal experience – convinced me that I needed to find a way to stop arguing with this writer and adopt a radically different approach to what he was trying to tell me.

In short, my problem was that I was contrasting every piece of new information with some long-held contrary opinion and challenging every new insight with an argument. Reacting that way to a book that was trying to tell me my mind was the problem (rather than the solution) was clearly not going to be very fruitful.

Or, as one of my friends remarked at the time: "You can't solve the problem *with* the problem."

Indeed.

So, over the course of the next 200 pages, rather than reacting with an aggressive argument every time I caught myself with a negative reaction, I forced myself to adopt a completely different approach by asking: "Where would this guy have to be standing to *see* things this way?" "What must his experiences be like for him to *feel* that way?"

It's hard to say how liberating this was. I suddenly found myself in a relatively calm, respectful dialogue with Eckhart Tolle rather than constantly plunging into one raging argument after another.

This is not to say that this approach allowed me to always "see things that way". Sometimes, I just couldn't figure out "where" Tolle was standing. At other times, when I did begin to get a better understanding of his position, I found his perspective completely alien to my own experience and/or my deeply held (but now judiciously reconsidered) beliefs.

Still, the exercise of compassionate listening rather than reactively arguing changed my experience with the book and – most important – eventually allowed me to significantly modify some of my long-held beliefs about myself and about the world.

This more inclusive, open-minded approach has fruitfully informed almost all of my reading since then. There is so much more I can learn from a dialogue rather than engaging in a smugly superior dead-end argument – especially with authors who are clearly smarter than me or who have had experiences that transcend my own.

Arguing rarely changes anyone's mind – most especially mine.

19.

"Future-back planning"

DURING THE LAST six years of my corporate career, I was privileged to work for a brilliant CEO named Mohan. (He is my final entry into the "three smartest people I've ever met" category already mentioned here.) Over and above his brilliant "outside the box" and visionary thinking, Mohan was inspiring, challenging and insightful in ways that I found to be profoundly impressive.

I *loved* working for this man!

Two fundamental elements in Mohan's very successful management style were: (1) the assignment of *measurable* goals along with (2) *concrete* and *reasonable* deadlines for reaching those goals. Once you were assigned a job, there was rarely any question about what you were being asked to do along with the definite date for accomplishing that goal.

This is a fairly common – although frequently ignored or forgotten – management technique, but Mohan improved on this by adding one more important tool to this basic model. He would teach his leadership team how to use what he called "future-back planning" – a practical way to ensure that you would meet your goal on time – and he encouraged them to spread this practice farther down the corporate ladder to the managers and sales people who worked for them.

Future-back planning requires you to break down the assigned goal into the individual steps you need to take to reach that goal. Once these are clearly identified, evaluated and understood, each step is then assigned its own attainable completion date. This creates an *ongoing* metric for tracking progress as the *final* deadline approaches.

There were hundreds of success stories from people in our company using this technique, but I have found the best way to explain the amazing effectiveness of future-back planning is to remind people of how the successful implementation of many, many incremental steps got us to the moon on time.

On May 25, 1961, President John F. Kennedy announced his vision of putting a man on the moon by the end of the decade. Kennedy knew that thousands and thousands of problems would have to be solved – scientific, technical, political and financial problems – but he didn't try to resolve them all in advance. What he did was to set a definite goal with a firm timetable and then authorized others to work out exactly what steps were needed so that his goal could be accomplished on time.

Supervised by NASA over the next eight years – throughout the end of the Mercury Project and on into the life of the Gemini and Apollo Projects – politicians along with scientists, technicians, inventors, consultants and astronauts all contributed to ensure that each individual step needed to reach this ambitious goal was accomplished on schedule.

And it worked! On July 20, 1969, the LEM (Lunar Excursion Module) landed safely on the moon and, a few hours later, Neil Armstrong climbed down the ladder to take his "one giant leap for mankind."

It's a perfect example of future-back planning!

But, the day-to-day applications of future-back planning isn't even close to the rocket science needed to get us to the moon. In most cases, it's just a matter of 'doing the math' and then acting on those results.

Here's just one example. Let's say that your company goal is for each salesperson to sell five of "X" every month. The first thing that salesperson needs to do is track and determine how many of their cold calls = how many official presentations = how many actual sales.

If it takes five cold calls (on average) to get one real presentation, and only one in four of those presentations (on average) resulted in a sale THEN to get five new sales of "X" each month your monthly metric for success would be 100 cold calls = 20 presentations = 5 sales.

THEN... given that there are roughly 20 business days in each month, each salesperson would need to make 5 cold calls every day to reach that number of 100 sales calls a month. Every day... no matter what! (*Or... at least, on average.*)

Whenever friends ask for business advice, my recommendations almost always include this basic formula of measurable goals, concrete deadlines and a future-back approach to daily planning. Unfortunately, many people just don't see the benefit of this simple approach, thinking that their business problems call for a much more complicated solution – which is rarely the case.

Perhaps my favorite success story is my friend, Chris, a salesman of used office equipment who decided to start his own business in the same field. Several months into this ambitious venture, he realized that he was just not selling enough product to make his new business successful. Failure loomed on the horizon.

We sat down and went over the numbers. Chris knew his target goal, which – taking into account a number of other relevant factors – was how many dollar's worth of equipment he needed to sell in a year. My first instinct was to take that number and divide it by 12 months, but he objected that his business was seasonal – so that kind of a simplistic approach wasn't going to work here.

"OK," I said. "Let's take you desired annual sales number and break them down into different monthly goals based on your hot, warm, cool and cold seasons." That done, each month's goal was divided by 20 business days to arrive at the daily sales goal. Then Chris told me that he was – again for a variety of solid reasons – more successful with his morning calls than he was in the afternoon. "How much more successful in the morning?" I asked. "Twice as successful," he replied confidently. So, we re-apportioned each daily sales target along those lines.

Chris loved having these concrete numbers in front of him every morning – telling him exactly what his sales targets were for that day. And it worked! His business flourished and grew *because* he paid careful and constant attention to the future-back metrics and their deadlines.

Future-back planning… It really isn't rocket science and it can certainly help ensure success whenever you are faced with a challenging business goal. NOTE: It also works when you are faced with challenging personal goals – like running a marathon or reading *Moby Dick*.

Thanks Mohan!

20.

Read some poetry

I WAS EDUCATED at a time when schools typically taught a fair amount of poetry and frequently insisted that we memorize poems as part of our homework. I was never a huge fan, but there were a few poems that have caught my attention and impressed me over the years. Who, for instance, wouldn't be captivated by the rhythm and rhymes of Edgar Allen Poe's "The Raven" or his lyrical "Annabel Lee."

Some of these memorized lines stuck with me throughout the years. I know that I haven't gone through a single spring without silently noting Shakespeare's "Rough winds do shake the darling buds of May..." on several occasions or an autumn without reciting to myself Gerard Manley Hopkin's lines, "Margaret are you grieving / Over Goldengrove unleaving?"

My dad, although he never made it past the 7th grade, was similarly loaded with these snippets of poetry memorized in his youth; occasionally proclaiming out loud things like "Who has seen the wind / Neither I nor you..." or "Under the spreading chestnut tree / The village smithy stands...".

In my late teens and early 20s, I was fascinated by a few select poems. At one point, I memorized every word of "The Love Song of J. Alfred Prufrock" because I was so completely intoxicated with the way Eliot put his words together. That poem just sang to me.

But the practice of reading poetry faded once I entered my mid-20s and didn't return for years.

Then, in my mid-40s, I met, courted and married the Lady Sara, who had been writing poetry since she was a child. She would often mention the names of modern poets in one context or another and, when I told her I had never heard of that person, she would just as frequently comment: "Well... she (or he) is *VERY* famous!" (Well... not in my world they weren't!)

The same year that we married, 1993, Janet Malcolm wrote a long, three-part article in *The New Yorker* on Sylvia Plath entitled "The Silent Woman". Sara encouraged me to read it and, in the magazine's sidebars, I got my first real exposure to Plath's amazing poems.

It was "Tulips" that first completely captivated me and I became a devoted fan. I was knocked out by its candor and emotional power. This was a woman that I wanted to spend more time with and, over the next year or so, I managed to read most of her published poems.

But I can't say that this revelation of Plath's brilliant, enlightening and engaging poetry set me off on a course of diligent exploration for more of the same. The few times that I did dip into the writings of one of those "very famous" people Sara would mention to me, I usually came away extremely disappointed. All too often, the readings proved to be difficult – if not incomprehensible – they were far too much work with far too little return. *Where's the fun in that?*

Besides Plath, T. S. Eliot continued to intrigue and delight me. Some of his poems make beautiful music in my head – with words rather than notes. Eliot can be *very* challenging in relation to his *exact* meaning and for that reason he is not recommended to all. But meaning wasn't primarily why I read his poems. It was the sheer lyricism of his writing that almost never failed to impress and please me. I found it to be positively hypnotic.

Once I started meditating on a regular basis, I was advised to do a short reading every morning from some "spiritual" or "inspirational" literature before sitting. I was told this was a good way for me to get into a proper "zone" of awareness before meditating. A few years into this practice, I discovered that reading sections of Eliot's "Four Quartets" in the mornings almost always took me there. I returned to them again and again because – for all their challenge, and, perhaps, because of it – I *really* love those poems. Could there be a better way to start an "insight" meditation sit than:

> We shall not cease from exploration
> And the end of all our exploring
> Will be to arrive where we started
> And know the place for the first time.

Over the years, I've tried a number of others poets with mixed results. But recently, I discovered the wonderful writings of Mary Oliver. Her poems are completely accessible, always lyrical and they deliver a message that I need to hear with regularity: *"Get out of your head, William, and get into a personal up-close relationship with the world around you!"* This book is prefaced with perhaps my favorite quote from Oliver, taken from the final three lines of "The Summer Day". After describing in wonder-filled detail her up-close encounter with a grasshopper, Mary brilliantly concludes:

> ...I don't know exactly what a prayer is.
> I do know how to pay attention, how to fall down
> into the grass, how to kneel down in the grass,
> how to be idle and blessed, how to stroll through
>   the fields,
> which is what I have been doing all day.
> Tell me, what else should I have done?
> Doesn't everything die at last, and too soon?
> Tell me, what is it you plan to do
> with your one wild and precious life?

Adding to my store of favorite poets over the years, my Lady Sara has written hundreds of haikus *(3-line poems of 5/7/5 syllables each)* during her morning meditation walks on the beach near our home. Last year, a family friend encouraged several of us to select our favorites and she had them privately published in a small book. These are just four of those that I love most:

> My blood this salt smell,
> my flesh this tidal mud, my
> soul a plaintive gull.

The heart lives outside
of time. And feels what it feels.
Answers to no one.

Be present, he said,
while you walk. But sometime, my
past walks beside me.

Let's start over, says
the world, after a rainy
night. Pretend I'm new.

    Try reading some poetry. I suspect it just might prove to be good for you soul.
    What's to lose?

21.

Whatever it is... just say "Welcome!"

THIS IS A fairly recent insight for me, but it requires quite a bit of a backstory to make any sense. I was raised Roman Catholic and only ever attended Catholic schools. After high school, I spent two years in the seminary studying to be a priest, but I fell into a doctrinal dispute with the Church and left when I was 19-years old. By the time I turned 22, I was completely areligious.

I live in a world that is positively filled with mystery, but without any supernatural elements or explanations – no ghosts or goblins, no spirits or souls, no gods or goddesses, no angels or devils, no heaven or hell – so I could be pretty critical when it comes to the whole idea of prayer. Given the chance, I would often scornfully quote Jim Morrison's line: "You cannot petition the Lord with prayer!"

Once, as already noted in Chapter 4, I was pompously expounding this point of view and my best friend, King – a man of nuanced and frequently indeterminate beliefs – had had enough. He noted that while there might not be *Someone* listening and responding to prayerful petitions, that fact in no way discounted the value of getting on your knees daily. King called it "assuming the position of humility" and he claimed it was the only appropriate response to the awe and anxiety we all feel when honestly acknowledging the realities of the human condition.

I always had tremendous respect for King's "spirituality" – so his advice carried particularly heavy weight with me. Although I couldn't bring myself to "petition the Lord with prayer" on a daily basis, there was no reason I couldn't take this suggestion and start getting on my knees every day and reciting – out loud – a list of positive affirmations. I came to think of this practice as the "story I tell myself" every morning about the person I was hoping to be that day.

While my original list was pretty short, it grew over the years because I felt the only way to keep it meaningful and vital, was to regularly update it. At one point it was two typed pages long, but today – after a recent major rewrite – it is back down to less than a single sheet of paper.

Over the past thirty-five years, I have rarely missed a morning when I didn't get on my knees.

The challenge – at least in the beginning – was deciding what to *say* on my knees each morning. This proved to be a really stimulating exercise in personal honesty and authenticity. Exactly what was it that I wanted to commit to believing, to doing and to striving for each day? What were the regular and most pressing difficulties I faced each day that kept me from acting like the person I most wanted to be?

While many of the specifics changed over the years, the format quickly settled into two parts. In the first, I reminded myself of some things I currently believe (for instance: "Everything changes. Everything dies. Nothing is permanent. Nothing is eternal.") while the second half focused on my aspirations for myself throughout the coming day ("I want to pause thoughtfully before speaking and to be aware of my tone").

Which brings us, finally, to "Welcome!" *(Sorry for the long backstory!).*

For at least twenty-five years, I have opened and closed my morning affirmations with the line: "Good morning to this day... and to everything that this day holds for me *personally* – WELCOME!"

I think of that 'welcoming' as the essence of all the "let it go" or "let it be" prayers ever recited by believers. It's not about Stoic endurance. Whatever this day holds for me... just bring it on and I will do my best to happily *embrace* it! *WELCOME!*

The problem was that while saying this faithfully every morning for decades, I would just as regularly forget to *DO* that welcoming-thing mere minutes after I got up off my knees. The classic story I have told against myself for a number of years was reciting the "Welcome to everything!" mantra one morning, and then going directly back to the bathroom and cutting myself while shaving – only to curse and swear loudly about the stupidity and the injustice of it all.

So much for "Welcome!"

I successfully ignored this complete lack of "follow through" for years while simultaneously overlooking the blatant hypocrisy of continuing to repeat that "Welcome!" statement every morning. But, whenever I *did* happen to notice this glaring discrepancy, I had to admit that I had made absolutely no substantive progress with moving my acceptance/embracing game forward in all those years.

Then, a couple of years ago, as I once again admitted to myself the complete lack of meaningful impact this affirmation was having on my day-to-day life, I realized it was time to DO something about it. My friend King had always emphasized positive actions (rather than lofty thoughts or fervent emotions) and so I resolved to take an action. I promised myself that I would say the word "Welcome!" out loud every time I caught myself having a negative reaction to something.

The first few days of doing this were a revelation to me. I found I was saying "Welcome!" *a lot*. Sometimes I could actually feel myself welcoming whatever was going on (my growing forgetfulness, for instance) while at other times, I was just saying the word without much real conviction (for instance, when confronted with computer problems). But, however much sincerity I might or might not bring to the "Welcome!", the result was always the same. By actually *doing* it, I gained a brighter awareness of what was actually going on in my life and within me *along with* the distinct feeling of having successfully dialed down (at least a bit!) whatever level of distress I was feeling at the time.

I realized that this "Welcome!" thing was just a shorter and more useful repackaging of the great Buddhist teacher Charlotte Joko Beck's definition of the Pali word *dukkha* (which is usually translated by the severely limited English word "suffering"). In response to a student's confusion over that word, Joko once explained: "Any time you say to yourself 'It shouldn't be this way'... that's *dukkha*".

These days, whenever I catch myself saying "Welcome!" it's always because I am thinking to myself "It shouldn't be this way!" Welcome! *Welcome!* WELCOME!!

22.

What is the "cash value" of your ideas and beliefs?

I AM A big fan of the American psychologist/philosopher William James. His most important works include *The Principles of Psychology* (1890), *The Varieties of Religious Experience* (1902), *Pragmatism* (1907) and *The Meaning of Truth* (1909). James was an original thinker who borrowed some contemporary philosophical trends from England and evolved them into "Pragmatism" – a uniquely American contribution to philosophy.

Many of James' ideas still excite controversy and none more so than his definition of truth. While arguments can be made for and against the broad application of his ideas on truth, I have always appreciated the clear and simple challenge he offered to the things that I *claim* to believe:

> Pragmatism asks its usual question. "Grant an idea or belief to be true," it says, "what concrete difference will its being true make in anyone's actual life? How will the truth be realized? What experiences will be different from those which

> would obtain if the belief were false? What, in short, is the truth's cash-value in experiential terms?"
>
> *Pragmatism* (p. 200)

James received mountains of grief for presenting one of his most important ideas in such colloquial American English, but he stuck by the metaphor of "cash-value" in book after book because he felt it most effectively communicated the kind of "truth" he was advocating for.

> It is astonishing to see how many philosophical disputes collapse into insignificance the moment you subject them to this simple test of tracing a concrete consequence... The whole function of philosophy ought to be to find out what definite difference it will make to you and me, at definite instants of our life, if this world-formula or that world-formula be the true one.
>
> *Pragmatism* (pp. 49-50)

You may struggle with some of that early 20th century prose, but, if the sentences are read slowly and carefully, William James' message is crystal clear. He asks: Do the things that you say you believe, have any real "cash value" in your life? Do they translate into concrete actions? Do they have an observable impact on how you behave throughout the day? Can they be seen in your reactions to life and in your daily interactions with others?

James' stunning challenge – insisting that I must actually live my beliefs out loud – forever leaves behind the confusing, sterile world of philosophical metaphysics and plants me firmly in the world of practical Reality.

'So, are you all talk,' he wants to know, 'or do your actions truly stand as a constant testimony to your beliefs?'

James' question makes me uncomfortable just about every time I think of it. It is similar to the stark emphasis 20th century existentialists put on "authenticity." But how "authentic" can I actually be once I realize that one of my cherished beliefs has no "cash-value" whatsoever?

If I am honest, it is a challenge that calls into question many of my spiritual, political, economic and social justice beliefs. And, if I'm not acting as if those beliefs were true... then what? Are they no more than lofty ideals and pious platitudes that have no real meaning, no real impact on my day-to-day life?

One concrete example of this can be seen in the "Welcome!" chapter above. It took me a long time – a couple of decades – before I honestly noticed and then owned the hypocrisy of daily professing something as a goal without making any real effort to actually put it into practice.

But once I noticed that blatant hypocrisy in a way that I could no longer ignore – who knows what triggered that sudden awakening to my oh-so comfortable duplicity? – I was forced to admit that I was being flagrantly dishonest telling myself that story, over and over again every morning.

Given that realization, I knew I had to either stop parroting that worthless daily affirmation, OR I had to make an honest attempt to change my behavior. In this case, I had to start saying "Welcome!" out loud to unpleasant and annoying things as they happened to me throughout the day.

It was either 'give it up' or 'give it some cash-value' and I have been actively trying to give it some real cash value since the day I realized and embraced my lack of real commitment to that "Welcome!" thing.

That is certainly one good example of how William James helped push me into action (finally!), but not all of my stories end on such a positive note.

For years, I've told my wife, my friends and, most of all, myself that, several times a week, I would go walking on the beach near our house. It's my only form of exercise (mild though it may be) and it's tremendously enjoyable whenever I manage to do it. There was one summer, more than fifteen years ago, when I walked on the beach several times a week for months – so I know it can be done. But, despite all my springtime promises and summertime protestations over the past decade and a half, I've rarely managed to take a beach walk more than five or six times during the summer.

In short, NO cash-value.

So, rather than continuing to be embarrassed by my repeated – and fairly public – failures in this regard, I simply stopped telling myself and others that these beach walks are going to happen. I stopped making those promises because they had no cash-value.

But either way – as a prompt to corrective action or as an incentive towards greater self-honesty – I am grateful to

William James for insisting that I need to hold myself to a higher standard.

It has most certainly helped make me and my beliefs and my life more authentic.

23.

"I am constitutionally incapable of being honest with myself, about myself, by myself"

I'VE ALREADY MENTIONED that my friend King was one of the best sources for excellent advice over the years. But he was so much more than that!

Seven years after graduating college, I felt the need to get the 'grey matter' working a bit more diligently, so I signed up for a night class on Aristotle at the local university. That's where I met King and I soon realized he was the best teacher I had ever met. I took classes from him whenever he taught at night, and building on our mutual interest in philosophy, we gradually became fast friends.

As our friendship grew, I was frequently surprised by the depth and clarity of King's insights – not only in relation to philosophy (which were *always* amazing!), but also regarding the more mundane realities of day-to-day life. In that area, I don't think I was ever more surprised than the first time I heard him casually say that he was "constitutionally incapable of being honest with himself, about himself, by himself."

Actually, I laughed out loud. I was sure he was making a joke. After all, he was perhaps the most self-aware and self-honest person I knew... so it had to be joke. Right?

Wrong! King's point was that as human beings, we are all innate "story-tellers". We constantly create stories to "make sense" of what our five senses tell us and those stories then evolve into and interact with our most cherished concepts and beliefs. Many (if not most) of them, self-serving.

His observation about being "constitutionally incapable" of being honest about himself was just a candid acknowledgement of how much his self-centeredness constantly colored the stories he told himself about how well or how poorly he was doing in life. The more the ego was involved – something he believed to be absolutely unavoidable – the more self-deception there was.

Given that problem, King believed that the best solution – i.e. the only way to get his stories edged just a little bit closer to Reality – was by openly vetting them with other people. Based on that understanding, he adopted the practice of candidly sharing his thoughts, his feelings, what he was doing and the motives for those actions with others on a regular basis.

For my friend, that insight and practice wasn't any more complicated than the admission that his self-perceptions could always be improved by "a second opinion" and he built up a small circle of understanding friends whom he regularly relied upon for helpful suggestions – a circle into which I was eventually granted membership.

Despite an upbringing that strongly emphasized the wisdom of keeping things to yourself, I began to adopt this practice for myself – starting with King. Then, like my friend, I slowly identified a few other friends who could be counted on to have the courage to "tell me the truth" whenever necessary.

Now, that may sound a bit ominous and onerous to people who were raised to be closed-mouth (even secretive) about their thinking, their feelings and their actions. But for me it is really nothing like that. At bottom, it is just a matter of getting in the habit of saying out loud – in the company of a trusted and perceptive friend(s) – the things that are going around and around in my head. It constantly amazes me how things that make perfect sense when I am thinking them – sometimes for days on end – can sound so disjointed or downright ridiculous once I start to say them out loud.

When I first adopted this practice, I was caught out more than a few times telling stories laced with self-pity – not a very attractive characteristic on the best of days and even worse once the self-pity had been pointed out to me on more than just a few occasions.

As I became more aware of what I was doing and how self-serving those stories were, I told them – and came to believe them – less and less. But, once I got those "bad" self-pity stories under control, they were frequently replaced by ones portraying me as the victim of whatever circumstances plagued me at the moment. I, of course, didn't actually *SAY* I was the *victim* in these situations, but it was hard to deny once that was pointed out to me. "Oh, so there's nothing you can do about that? It's completely beyond your control? So, you're just the victim here, is that it?"

One recent Friday provides an example. I am a technologically-challenged old guy on the best of days and this particular morning I was confronted with four (FOUR!) separate technology failures: the high-speed internet was running at one-third capacity, I was blocked from getting into my online Spam folder, we could NOT set up my wife's new iPhone and, when that problem was finally resolved, she couldn't send or receive emails. By 2 PM, I was in a serious meltdown.

While I wanted to go into my "why do these things always happen to me?" routine, I had come to learn how self-indulgent that statement was. Still, I often find it extremely challenging not to take these impersonal things very personally. So, as we drove the 15 miles *back* to the Apple store for professional help, I told Sara not only about how badly I was doing (this was *no* surprise to her), but also how hard I was trying to "dial it back"... without any success. I was working very hard to do that "Welcoming!" thing, but I wasn't believing a word of it! Telling her that out loud didn't solve my problem, but it did let her know that I wasn't just 'running' with it. I was actively trying to be less of a frustrated, angry jerk – however little results she might be seeing from all those efforts.

The next day, I told my friend, Ray, about the previous day's melt down and about how little success I had trying to control the stress and the anger. He just laughed and told me it was about time I'd had at least one really challenging day. Then we talked about what stories I might have been telling myself that made the situation worse than it had to be – most especially the ones where I tell myself these things are all being directed at me *personally*. I am frequently reminded of a motivational talk I heard years ago where the speaker said: "Traffic doesn't care!" Oh, you mean it's *not* about me?

My Lady Sara is firmly on board with this whole program of sharing to lessen our self-deception, but rather than referencing King, she likes to quote that other great philosopher, Winnie the Pooh, who noted: "...when you are a Bear of Very Little Brain, and you Think of Things, you find sometimes that a Thing which seemed very Thingish inside you is quite different when it gets out into the open and has other people looking at it." (*The House at Pooh Corner*, p. 102) Indeed!

Amen, Pooh Bear, and a big THANK YOU to King!

A template for questioning the veracity of my self-perceptions (*"Don't believe everything you think!"*) may be the greatest gift you ever gave me.

24.

"Become a morning person!"

For several years, I organized and moderated a Leadership Academy within our company. Every year, twenty students who had exhibited their potential for significant growth were selected for this honor. Over the course of the next two years, they attended nine days of classes and spent three days interning with an executive mentor whom they had selected from within the company.

Based on the belief that business education is best taught by people with practical, real-life experience, all of the speakers at the Academy were successful company executives who were asked to do presentations and run workshops based on their particular areas of expertise.

I frequently called upon my friend, Dilo, to fill several of these teaching slots. He was not only one of the most prominent rising stars within the company, he was also a gifted communicator and a dynamic teacher. The twenty students who sat around that u-shaped classroom table all hoped that they might someday be as successful as Dilo, so whenever he spoke, they listened with rapt attention.

During those years, Dilo was what we called a "division president" (there were about 40 of these in the company at the time). But his success continued to grow exponentially over the years and today Dilo is the CEO of that company.

Included in the "wrap up" sessions during the final day of Leadership Academy, Dilo always did a presentation on "What Will I Do Tomorrow" which suggested twelve practical strategies that the students should adopt if they hoped to become really successful within the company.

All of these suggestions were fairly specific to a typical business environment ("Be a mentor, coach, quarterback" and "Guard your present customers with your life!"), but the one that always caught my attention was "Become a morning person!". This was an important piece of *universal* advice, a suggestion applicable not only to my own business career, but also to every other aspect of my life.

Dilo admitted that many people identified themselves as "night owls", claiming that they did their best work at the end of the day, but he would have none of it and he was pretty passionate about this! If you want to be successful in business and in most any other endeavor you attempt in your life, he said, the morning would always be the time slot where you would make the most progress towards accomplishing your goals.

And he offered some practical questions for anyone who was trying to adopt this advice: "Review how you spend your time in the evening. What are you doing then that gets in the way of you being a morning person? Could any of those activities be eliminated, modified or moved to the morning? What time do you normally go to bed?" He also suggested a critical review of your typical morning habits: "What time do you normally get up every day? What is it you actually do every morning? What, if any of those things, could be eliminated."

In short, how could you rearrange things so that you could be less distracted, more focused, and therefore more productive every morning?

Having made these vital assessments, Dilo confidently claimed that adopting a set of new habits so that you were up and being more productive in the morning would seriously impact the level of your success in the company and in many of the other things you might want to accomplish in your life.

I have always had jobs that required me to be present at work in the morning. Despite this, during most of my business career, I most definitely considered myself to be a "night owl" – someone whose productivity didn't really kick in until sometime after dinner.

When I retired, I found myself 'sleeping in' many mornings, but I soon began to notice just how unproductive my days were under that regimen. Remembering Dilo's advice, I began to make a concerted effort to shut the television off and go to bed earlier each night. This, coupled with the new practice of setting an alarm so that I got up at an early hour, proved to be extremely beneficial. Suddenly, I was getting more and more things on my daily "to-do" list crossed off by the end of the day.

In my case, I credit this to the lack of distractions in the morning. Nobody calls, emails or texts early in the morning, and this allowed me to concentrate on whatever I put my mind to without any interruptions. My productivity skyrocketed so significantly that there was no way I could argue with the fact that my attempt to "become a morning person" was having a tremendously positive effect on my life and on my daily sense of accomplishment.

Who knew such a small change in my habits could have such a profound effect on my life!

And I was not the only one in the family to adopt this advice. After my Lady Sara retired, she had similar experiences with 'sleeping in' in the mornings. "The day was gone before I knew it," she said and could only wonder "Where did it go?"

Her answer to that question was to get out of bed earlier every morning. She began to regularly get up just before dawn and go for walks down to the beach near our house. The sunrise pictures that she so frequently took were amazing! And, it was also on those walks that Sara started writing haikus *(those small 3-line poems of 5/7/5 syllables each)*.

Over the years, I recorded well over a hundred of these and – as noted in Chapter #20 – several of them were later privately published in a small book for friends.

None of that would ever have happened unless Sara had made a commitment to be "a morning person" and I would have missed the opportunity to read, collect and then share these lovely haikus with you:

> Peaceful morning. I
> need quiet. It nourishes
> me. Breathe it like air.

My awakened self
exists within. All day I
try to see its face.

Morning riches. Sun
jewels on the horizon.
all day I'll spend them.

No one in his right
mind is out, so I walk in
mindless solitude

Who would want to miss that experience – both walking and writing and then afterwards reading?

Become a morning person!!

25.

"Only you can do it... but you can't do it alone"

Sometime later, I realized that King's defense against his problem of self-centered thinking – the inclusion of other people – could be fruitfully applied to so many other areas of my life. I have no idea where I first heard the paradoxical statement noted above, but it perfectly captures a much broader application of my friend's reliance on other people... one that can certainly contribute to a more flourishing life. As they say, "it takes a village" and it's *good* to be a part of a village.

And this is where the advice from two of the "smartest" people I ever met dramatically clashed and contradicted each other.

For years, our former therapist, Larry, and I would meet every three months for lunch. At times, our conversations could be a bit contentious – after all, there's nothing wrong with a good argument! – but it took me a while to identify the "fork in the road" where we always parted ways.

It turned out that Larry – along with just about every other psychiatrist, psychologist or therapist I have ever met – believed that the proper goal of personal therapy was to help their clients become more *autonomous*. Although he never said it quite so categorically, Larry believed that mature mental health was defined by the ability to "stand on your own two feet." *Ideally*, people were supposed to be self-reliant, self-directed and independent.

This pursuit of autonomy as the individual's highest goal flew directly in the face of all the advice I was receiving from King – who regularly and successfully leaned on his circle of friends for mental, emotional, intellectual and spiritual support.

The more my own experience confirmed the benefits of a communitarian approach, the more I came to believe that Larry's primary focus on autonomy was a classic example of "picking up the wrong end of the stick." Certainly, we are responsible for our own lives, but to hold up autonomy and self-reliance as the paramount goal of personal development completely eliminates any possibility of accessing the wealth of wisdom and support so readily available from others.

Not to mention the undeniable fact that a mindless pursuit of idealized independence all too often leads to anxious feelings of separation and, at times, debilitating isolation, alienation and depression.

My own experience strongly confirms that autonomy isn't the solution. In fact, I believe that this doggedly sole reliance on autonomy – without being judiciously tempered by some positive dependence on others – is the source of many of our problems today. We *are* communal animals!

In short, my disagreements with Larry grew out of his insistence that autonomy was the preferred foundational goal for human beings while consistently denigrating most any form of dependence as either a 'bad' or, at best, as an 'unhealthy' life choice. (He would surely have laughed at the way the Lady Sara and I regularly describe our relationship as "happily co-dependent.")

When did "dependence" ever get such a bad name?

For one thing, telling people that you need help because you "can't do it alone" flies directly in the face of our Western – and, most especially, our American – culture. Over the past few centuries, self-reliance and autonomy have slowly grown to be the West's highest and most desirable values. They are so deeply ingrained into our basic emotional framework that it's hard to even notice them. They form the foundation of our self-conceptions, drive our introspective self-evaluations and typically serve as the yardstick for all of our feelings of self-worth.

Older Americans often think of this as the "John Wayne" syndrome; the ideal of being so self-sufficient that you *never* need anyone's help OR if you *do* need help – however desperate that need might be – you wouldn't ask for it because the blow to your pride and ego would be just too painful.

In contrast to this obsessively individualistic approach to life, "only you can do it... but you can't do it alone" suggests the possibility of a middle way: a life-path where personal responsibility and accountability remain intact while still being informed and judiciously moderated by the acknowledged need of some help from others. In short, "interdependence" isn't something that must necessarily be seen as negative, something to be avoided as a vice or an abject admission of failure. Instead, it can be recast and recognized as the very positive virtue of "being connected".

I was deeply infected with this Western doctrine of self-reliance and independence during my 20s and 30s, aspiring – with far more hubris than I realized at the time – to be an exemplar of the "lonely genius" model. (Reading a lot of Nietzsche at an early age can be hazardous!) Today, I am profoundly embarrassed when I think about many events from that phase of my life.

As I entered my 40's, I began to get a glimpse of a much richer version of life that would be available to me if only I adopted a more "collective" approach. A few years later, I met and married the Lady Sara who helped me to exponentially increase my embrace of a life of greater connectedness.

Here's just one example of how this has worked for us. Although Sara claims to be much more retiring than me, she cooked dinner for eight to ten of our friends every Monday night for 30 years – a practice that only ended with the COVID lockdown. A few of those friends came every week for all three decades while others – who had moved away or died – were replaced by more recent acquaintances. Our Monday night dinners were the scene of heartfelt confessions and raucous 'inventory taking' – in short, a forum where each of us could candidly share our lives and gratefully acknowledge that only we could do it, but we just couldn't do it alone.

Those dinners were legendary and a stellar example of the beauty and the joy of interdependence!

Meditation 17
by John Donne *[1623]*

No man is an island, entire of itself;
Every man is a piece of the continent, a part of the main.

If a clod be washed away by the sea, Europe is the less,
As well as if a promontory were, as well as if a manor of thy
friend's or thine own were.

Any man's death diminishes me,
because I am involved in mankind;
And therefore, never send to know for whom the bell tolls;
It tolls for thee.

26.

"You need to have the conversation before the conversation…"

OVER THE COURSE of several couple counselling sessions, our therapist offered us a number of pieces of outstanding advice and one of the most important and life-changing was this suggestion about the need to have "the conversation *before* the conversation". As noted earlier, Larry believed that almost all relationship problems could be traced back to bad communication and he had convinced us that silence (i.e. the *lack* of any communication) was the greatest enemy of maintaining a good relationship.

This is an interesting, insightful and extremely helpful diagnosis of the problem, but learning how to actually communicate more effectively proved to be a much more challenging task.

Larry's best advice in this area was that we should always make room for a preemptory conversation before starting one of those "difficult" conversations that come up in every relationship.

So, if one of us wanted to discuss a "problem" issue – whatever it might be – he suggested that *before* launching into the topic at hand, the person initiating the conversation should begin by saying something like this:

> "Sara, I'd really like to talk about something, but I'm nervous about bringing it up. I'm worried that it might come out the wrong way and hurt your feelings and that is very last thing I would ever want to do."

Whenever I started a conversation with some variation of that kind of introduction, Sara's typical response was always positive – if, understandably, a bit guarded – encouraging me to go ahead and tell her whatever was on my mind.

Reassuring Sara that I was not about to thoughtlessly (or maliciously) hurt her feelings, allowed her to lower her natural defenses a bit – significantly reducing the chance of a knee-jerk negative reaction which might well have been the response, if I had just bull-dozed my way into my topic or complaint without any forewarning whatsoever.

Larry said that this kind of opening statement would reassure Sara that I wasn't about to carelessly attack her, or to dump a load of blame on her for some problem – real or imagined – in our relationship. Instead, I was clearly and compassionately inviting her to an open discussion – a dialogue – rather than offering what might otherwise be heard as the provocation for a fight.

The point of the conversation before the conversation, he said, was to remind ourselves that we were both "on the same side of the fence" – the best place to be when beginning a difficult conversation. Without that upfront reassurance, we might quickly assume that we were on "opposite sides of the fence" – a position that favors nothing so much as throwing rocks at each other.

Some couples seem to just thrive on confrontation. It's somehow built into their emotional and psychological DNA. And, for those people, frequent arguments seem to work.

But Sara and I are not one of those couples. We are both pretty averse to confrontation. Our default tendency is to say nothing rather than something – no matter what the provocation. But, as Larry was so fond of pointing out, this was nothing less than a self-administered dose of poison – one that we drank every time we remained silent about something that was bothering us.

All of which should explain why I have been known to say with some regularity that "the five most courageous things I've done in the last three decades have all started with the words: 'Sara there's something I'd like to talk about…'"

Saying that simple phrase terrifies me because once it's out of my mouth, the game is on! There is no turning back! The can of worms is about to be opened!

And the need for a little bit of emotional courage is completely appropriate here since experience has taught me that – despite my best efforts – I can never predict exactly where one of *those* conversations is going to go. With some regularity, it prompts Sara to say things about me that I would rather not hear or, worse-case scenario, the talk could go completely south and turn into a dreadful fight – something I would do almost anything to avoid.

And so, over the past three decades I have, on several occasions – following Larry's challenging, but very helpful advice – reassured my wife that there was something I wanted to talk about but that I was reluctant to bring up because...

"I'm worried I will hurt your feelings..."

"I'm afraid it will make you angry..."

"I'm worried that it may sound like I'm beating a dead horse..."

"I'm afraid it will shock you when I say..."

"I'm worried I might drive you away from me..."

"I'm afraid it will make you cry..."

Starting that way tells Sara that it is not my intention to attack or hurt her. On the contrary, I am *explicitly* saying that those are the last things I want to do and that I am hoping to avoid those results by doing my very best to say things in a way that will not trigger any of those dreaded reactions.

Again... such an opening is an invitation to a dialogue rather than an argument. It is an invitation to carefully, judiciously and respectfully put some difficult cards on the table – face up – and then *negotiate* how we can best resolve the conflicts and disagreements between them. (Another one of Larry's truism was that: "Loving someone doesn't mean you will always agree with them. You need to get over that belief!")

The conversation before the conversation makes perfect sense once the basic concept is understood; you are preparing the way for a difficult conversation by prefacing it with a loving and caring one.

It is one great piece of advice that I have found works amazingly well... whenever I have had the emotional courage to actually use it.

27.

Is It Skillful or Unskillful?

FOR WELL OVER a decade, I've been reading something from Buddhist literature almost every day and I have consistently been attracted to many of the perspectives I find there – ways of looking at things that are so very different from the way that I was raised to look at things.

One radically different way of approaching life's problems can be seen in the fact that the Buddha's teachings are so solidly grounded in *Immediate Reality*. People constantly asked him metaphysical questions, but he *always* refused to wander off into the abstract. His comments and instructions were consistently focused on the here and now, dealing only with those things that each of us can *directly experience* in our own lives.

I am particularly impressed by what might be called the underlying framework of his 'moral' teachings. Rather than diving into the age-old Western controversy about right and wrong and all the treacherous logical arguments surrounding the words "good" and "evil", the Buddha suggested that the most fruitful way to evaluate our personal actions would be to focus on whether they were "skillful" or "unskillful".

> Abandon what is unskillful, monks. It is possible to abandon what is unskillful... Because this abandoning of what is unskillful is conducive to benefit and pleasure, I say to you, "Abandon what is unskillful".
>
> Develop what is skillful, monks. It is possible to develop what is skillful... Because this development of what is skillful is conducive to benefit and pleasure, I say to you, "Develop what is skillful".
>
> Kusala Sutta, *Anguttara Nikaya* 2.19

Now, the 'packaging' of that ancient piece of advice is more than a little stilted, but the message is crystal clear. Rather than offering a dualistic, either/or moral perspective, the Buddha is recognizing the fact that my life as a living, breathing human being unfolds within a dynamic, ever-changing spectrum of possibilities. He isn't telling me what I *am*. Instead, he is pointing out a path with no absolutes – one that calls for the ongoing commitment to developing a life that is "skillful" and therefore "conducive to benefit and pleasure".

I have found this concrete, practical and nuanced way of assessing my actions very liberating because it is so far removed from the dualistic metaphysical world where everything is evaluated as either an absolute right or wrong, as an unequivocal good or evil, as positively spiritual or sinful.

This supremely practical way of judging my actions dovetails nicely with the Buddha's teaching about the fundamental "rightness" of my basic human nature. Suzuki Roshi (founder of the San Francisco Zen Center in 1962 and the man most directly responsible for the current flowering of Buddhism in the United States) once "explained" this belief by saying:

> Each of you is perfect the way you are ...
> and you can use a little improvement.
> Shunryu Suzuki,
> *To Shine One Corner of the World*, p. 3

This wonderfully laughable Zen evaluation not only provides a much gentler perspective on how I might better understand myself and my basic nature, it also presents me with the perfect rationale for extending compassionate understanding to everyone else I encounter in my life.

They too are perfect just the way they are, but, yes, they could *ALL* use a little bit of improvement!

It's hard to quantify the change that these two radically different and very positive perspectives have made in my life. "Huge" would be one way to put it. Having been raised in a practicing Roman Catholic household and a pre-Vatican II Catholic school environment, the messages I constantly received from both of those sources focused on the "sinfulness" of my actions and the "fallen" state of my nature.

Those beliefs – that I am a "fallen" creature and that I was born with an inherently "sinful" nature – are two foundational tenets of Christianity; explanations so deeply embedded in our traditional belief systems that it is almost impossible to "see" them. They are like the air we breathe – overlooked, unnoticed and completely taken for granted.

Centuries of reading Paul, Augustine and Calvin have firmly planted these two negative perspectives deeply into our secular Western ethos. It is, for instance, easy to see these same black-and-white perspectives in our political traditions where some politicians see our citizens as 'good people in need of legislative help,' while others see only a horde of liars, cheats and thieves that 'good people' need to be protected from.

Following our recent more relaxed cultural trends, Christian leaders in the second half of the 20th century have struggled mightily to counterbalance these traditionally negative beliefs by preaching a message heavily laden with "Love!" But this new emphasis on compassion and fellowship is invariably followed by prescriptions for personal improvement based on the same basic starting presumption – that we are intrinsically flawed, fallen, debased and sinful creatures.

The underlying premise of my upbringing was that the only choice was between Good or Evil. But that simplistic, dualistic, black-and-white understanding of human nature offered me a very limited range of options for change – almost all of which focused on the fact that I had to find a way to *rip out* those "defects of character" that were causing me (and the people around me) so much pain and grief.

Augustine famously prayed: "O Lord, help me to be pure... but not yet". Just how attainable is that perfection of 'purity' in the life of a typical person? I would suggest it is a recipe for failure. When the absolutist bar gets set so high, we realize the futility of it all and give up in despair. That is, if we even start trying in the first place.

How much better to accept the fact that these things are just a natural part of me, ones that are never going to go away, and work on developing some "skillful" means for dealing with them. That is, at least, an attainable goal and, when something "unskillful" occurs, the solution is clear: "Start again and try to develop something more skillful."

Best of all, this perspective on "skillful" and "unskillful" is an attitude that makes not only self-forgiving, but also compassionate forgiveness of others essential elements in my life.

And... what's not to like about that?

28.

"The difference between doing something and doing nothing is everything"

THE JESUIT PRIEST, Daniel Berrigan, was – among many other things – one of the most active and disruptive anti-war protesters during the Vietnam War era.

Perhaps most famously, he and his brother Philip (also a Jesuit) along with seven others Catholic protestors broke into the Catonsville MD draft board on May 17, 1968, dragged over 400 draft records out into the parking lot and publicly burned them. They were all arrested.

Berrigan was sentenced to three years in jail for this illegal action, but he went 'fugitive' in April of 1970 – the day before he was supposed to report to prison. He infuriated the FBI (who put him on the Most Wanted List – the only priest to ever earn that 'honor') by giving speeches to large crowds and then quickly disappearing. He was finally captured at a friend's house four months later and taken to jail.

This was, of course, the height of the war protest movement; a time of dramatic actions, high passions and – for some – even higher moral commitment.

Berrigan once famously summarized his own philosophy on commitment by stating:

> One cannot level one's moral lance at every evil in the universe. There are just too many of them. But you *can* do something, and the difference between doing something and doing nothing is everything.

I do not believe that Berrigan is suggesting the only way to survive in this world with our moral dignity intact is to adopt the kind of radical, controversial and consequential actions for which he and his brother were so famous. But I do believe his larger point is crystal clear and unassailable.

Namely, that unless we are willing to "do something" concrete in relation to whatever ethical issue happens to capture our attention (and the possibilities there are legion), then we are just not living up to our responsibilities as decent, caring, compassionate human beings.

Berrigan is not really asking that much of us. He is just suggesting that we do *something* rather than nothing – *whatever* that something might be. It doesn't have to be something as extreme as his own acts of defiance... it just has to be a decided *action* of some sort – however small.

One of the first things I learned when I began spending time with my Lady Sara was how generously she contributed to the causes that she felt passionate about. To cite just one example of many, she not only regularly donated money to a local woman's shelter, but, being a wholesale florist at that time, she would also regularly send them flowers to brighten up the house.

I quickly realized that I would have to "take my game up a notch or two" if I was going to earn this woman's respect and I began following her lead – admittedly for the most shallow of reasons... but then actions trump intentions every time!

And it has been an interesting and immensely rewarding journey for almost four decades now.

While making contributions to worthy organizations (such as a women's shelter) is certainly one way that I have consistently been "doing something" in Berrigan's terms, I found that I find it much more rewarding to help people on a one-to-one basis.

An activist friend and I occasionally argue over whether our efforts should (a) focus on pulling drowning people out of the river *one at a time* OR should we (b) try to identify *why* those people are in the river in the first place and then put our time and energy into correcting *that* situation.

This isn't an either/or argument – it's easily possible to be doing both things. But, on one level, I think it is about temperament more than anything else. Are you a person who prefers to deal with larger issues (Berrigan) or does working with needy individuals appeal more to you (me)?

I have always been impressed and challenged by the following little parable:

The day after a hurricane, the beach was littered with debris – most notably thousands of starfish that had been stranded by the rapidly receding waters.

As a man walked along the edge of the surf, he noticed someone up ahead who was throwing things out to sea. As he got closer, he realized it was a young woman laboriously picking up the starfish, one at a time, and flinging them back out into the water.

He stopped to chat and finally asked her: "So, just what do you think you're doing here?"

"I'm saving these starfish," she said.

"But, there are thousands and thousands of them dying here on the beach. What possible difference could it make?"

"Well," she said, "it makes all the difference in the world to this one," as she tossed yet another starfish back into the ocean.

While I do contribute to politically compatible candidates and to organizations working on problems and issues that I care about, the most satisfying "something" Sara and I have been doing over the past couple of decades are the small thing we can do to *directly* help struggling individuals.

Sometimes, these are friends or even just acquaintances in need. Everyone can use a helping hand at one time or another – be that financial, spiritual or emotional support. In addition, we have established satisfying connections in a nearby distressed community – for instance, pastors who know that they can come to us when something like $50 or $500 in cash could make all the difference in the world to someone who is truly in need.

The point for me has been that when I look at myself in the mirror, I know I can't claim to have solved any of the huge problems facing our world, but I do know that I have done "something" and, to quote Robert Frost, "that has made all the difference" to the man that I see staring back at me.

29.

"Tell me... what does your trend line look like?"

THE COMPANY RUN by my brilliant former boss, Mohan, was built by systematically acquiring potentially profitable family-run businesses and then "rolling them up" into one large efficient corporation. As already mentioned, the fundamental elements of his very successful management style was based on measurable goals, concrete deadlines and his technique of "future-back" planning (see Chapter #19).

But there was one other extremely important factor that Mohan always brought to those very specific goals and deadlines. If an executive was not hitting his assigned targets in a timely fashion, he would not belabored that failure. He didn't believe browbeating to be an effective management tool.

Instead, he would ask: "So... what does your trend line look like in relation to that missed goal... are you at least moving in the right direction with it?" If the trend line did, in fact, show some measurable progress towards the target goal, Mohan would typically praise the executive for whatever success they had manage to achieve and then ask them to explain the specific actions they had taken so far to move the needle in the right direction.

With that information in hand, he would then offer helpful suggestions for further actions (specific policies, procedures and programs) that – if put in place – would help accelerate progress towards that desired goal. These suggestions came, of course, with a new set of well-defined, attainable targets, each of which had its own concrete deadline for completion.

The most important goal that all our company's managers were tasked to achieve was a profit of 20% each month. Since these newly acquired family-run businesses were not currently operating on anything like that level of profitability, the former owners – now newly minted corporate executives – were almost immediately introduced to a set of simple, but comprehensive, financial skill sets they had previously lacked – skills that would be essential to their success in this new, larger, corporate environment.

This proved to be a very steep – and in some cases, impossible – learning curve for some of them. But for those who could show a trend line that was moving in the right direction, Mohan was always accommodating and encouraging. Besides providing a team of advisors well-versed in these financial tools, he would also ask the underperforming executive: "So tell me… what's getting in the way of your success here?" And, if there was anything he could do to remove or, at least, smooth out some of those "speed bumps" or "stop signs" his executive was experiencing, he would do so.

Mohan wasn't just a brilliant businessman. He was an amazing visionary, an inspiring leader and, even more important, an outstanding teacher.

I was brought up in a family (not to mention... an American culture!) that was solidly "either/or". The metric was **either** success **or** failure – there was no 'middle ground'.

But, having seen this "trend line" approach work time and time again within our company, I soon found myself adopting it into a number of other aspects of my life.

Mohan's business metrics showed me that I could recast the rigid, black-and-white value system that I was raised with into something more flexible; something that would allow me to see my life – and to *live* my life – from a more nuanced and forgiving perspective.

Of course, everything in life doesn't lend itself to this kind of measurement and control. You either get the "A" or you don't. You either make the team or you don't. You either ace that hole or you don't.

But there were a number of areas of my life where this proved to be immensely helpful... areas where I could generate some sort of guiding metric – *you can't have a trend line without collecting some supporting data* – that would tell me what kind of progress I was making (or not) in relation to some particular goal I had chosen.

This was certainly immensely helpful in relation to my writing projects.

While writing my last book, a notice popped up on my computer every Sunday at 8 AM asking: "So... how many pages did you write since last Sunday?" I would then write the total number of pages completed so far into a Word.doc along with the number of pages finished that week.

My goal was to write 8 pages a week, but there were weeks when I only got 2 written. Some other week, I might write 15 pages. But there were also weeks where NO new pages were written. Whatever happened, I noted the reason for the high, low or zero number – which was helpful in identifying what was and wasn't working for me in moving this project forward in a timely fashion.

And... the book did get finished. Not as quickly as I had originally planned. But it *was* finally all written, edited and published.

Some other goals could be tracked with less formal data collection. For instance, I get on the scale every morning and note my weight. This avoids those surprises when all of a sudden my clothes don't fit anymore and I realize I've gained 10 pounds while I wasn't paying attention!

These days, many of the new digital devices can be extremely helpful in establishing trend lines. My meditation app tells me how many days in a row I've meditated. Another app tells me how many steps I've taken each day... reminding me that I am or I am not getting out walking on a regular basis.

And... it's important to note that this "trend line" model has also been helpful to me when things are going in the other direction. Since my late 50s, I've noticed (and often grievously complained about) my increasing lack of ability to retrieve the name or the word that I'm trying to say out loud. For me this has been an ever-increasing problem – a downward trend line for the past three decades.

But noticing and acknowledging this as a normal and unavoidable symptom of aging is not just helpful, it's important. As my Lady Sara once told me after I had loudly complained about not being able to retrieve the word "refrigerator": "I don't mind that you can't think of a particular word sometimes," she said, "but what bothers me is that you get so angry about it!"

Indeed. The old age trend line is the old age trend line. Get over it, William!

30.

"Meditate! Every day!!"

THE "MEDITATION" WORD is so contaminated that most Western readers immediately imagine a robed figure sitting cross-legged on a cushion as they chant "Ooom!" over and over again.

Throw out that old conception!

NOTHING could be farther from the truth!

The suggestion that I meditate daily is easily the second most important piece of advice I have ever received – and then *finally* started doing – and I have my California friends, Jay and Adelle, to thank for introducing me to a daily practice of mindfulness.

These two "sit" daily and they had, on several occasions, tried to convince me to adopt a regular meditation practice. But I was resistant... in the extreme. So much so that during one frustrating conversation, Adelle scathingly commented: "Bill, you just can't get spiritually healthy and sane without a daily meditation practice!" (*Oh, yeah... well, just watch me!*)

Not only did they meditate together daily, every Thursday night they joined a non-denominational group of fellow meditators and, during my frequent West Coast business trips, Jay regularly tried to get me to attend this group with them.

Fortunately (*I thought*), I was almost never in California on Thursday night.

But finally, on Thursday, February 14, 2008, I happened to be in downtown Los Angeles setting up for a book fair and Jay volunteered to come by and pick me up for dinner. We got a quick bite in LA, but he then drove me all the way back to his home town of Manhattan Beach and dropped me right into the middle of that weekly meditation group.

What a revelation!

I was expecting a cultish "California thing", but here were these thirty-five perfectly normal people quietly meditating at the beginning and the end of their ninety-minute session and, in between, talking about the topic of the night – the books they were currently reading to help them with their practice. Jay apologized to me for "the small group" that night. "It's Valentine's Day", he said.

I was deeply moved and impressed and, back home, I talked pretty compulsively about it for the next two weeks to my wife and my friend King. Finally, I realized that I should stop talking about it and try some of this "quiet sitting" for myself.

The problem was that I didn't know a single person on the East Coast with a regular meditation practice. I called Jay and asked for a helpful book and he suggested I try Eckhart Tolle's *The Power of Now* – which I bought and started to read immediately. (See Chapter #18 for some details of my first encounters with this book.)

Jay was insistent that if I was going to do this, I had to commit to a daily practice. He was more than a little militant about that *daily* thing. He suggested a minimum of two 3-minute periods of silence each day and he drove this "advice" home by commenting: "And don't tell me you can't find six minutes somewhere in your day to be doing this!"

The Buddhist sage, Nagarjuna, made the same point (although a bit more cryptically): "Discipline," he said, "is the pathway to freedom". Indeed!

And so, my journey into mindfulness – into being more present in my life – began.

People meditate for a lot of different reasons. Some are searching for peace and serenity, others hope for new insights into themselves and the world around them. Some "just sit" in the Japanese style (zazen) hoping to reach satori – or Enlightenment or Nirvana as it is called by other Buddhist schools. Some people, like me, are just trying to be more present in their lives.

Long before I began meditating, I was aware that I spent far too much time in my head and almost no time in my body. I had noticed, for instance, that all too often I would arrive at the office and have no clear memory of the shower I had taken that morning or the cup of coffee that accompanied an equally unremembered breakfast. The blatant fact of the matter was that I hadn't *really been there* for any of those experiences because I was so thoroughly distracted by the plans and schemes that were running through my busy, busy mind all the time.

You mean I wasn't really *there* for that hot morning shower – one of the flat-out guaranteed pleasures of the day?

NO, I wasn't. I was somewhere else in my head and completely oblivious to the experience.

One of my favorite Buddhist teachers, Charlotte Joko Beck says: "The point of practice [i.e.. meditation] is to reduce the amount of time that we spend being absent, caught in our self-centered dream." For the past sixteen years, I have worked at solving that problem by sitting in silence every morning and most evenings; trying to *be* with my body and my breath while noting (but not engaging with) those "uninvited thoughts" that still constantly run through my busy head.

Sitting is my "practice" time for being as present as possible throughout the rest of the day.

We are all different and this is as true of meditation practices as it is of everything else in life. It's not just about someone sitting on a cushion and chanting "Ooom"!

It took me a fair amount of experimentation to find out *what worked best for me*. I started out with my eyes closed, but, a couple of years later, adopted the Zen practice of having them slightly open. In the beginning, I leaned back comfortably in a chair, then I learned to sit up straight. After a while, I migrated to a cushion and, finally, a few years later, arrived at today's kneeling bench. At times my meditations have been as short as five minutes and as long as an hour. Perhaps the only constant in my practice has been that I always read something 'spiritual' before sitting; a practice that consistently helps me to 'get into the zone' before meditating.

All of that is one way of stressing that there is no "right" way to sit, no "right" length of time to meditate, no "right" book to read. The important thing was that I continued experimenting until I found out what works best *for me* – while always honoring my commitment to do it daily.

This morning, to give just one example, I read my Daily Stoic book, a poem by Mary Oliver and a small bit from one of Meister Eckhart's sermons before sitting for 15 minutes. This evening, I will sit with my Lady Sara for 15 minutes after she reads a page or two aloud from Joko Beck's second book, *Nothing Special*.

Blaise Pascal commented in his *Pensées*: "All of men's miseries derive from not being able to sit in a quiet room alone".

Who wouldn't want some relief from that?

The Evening Gatha
(A Buddhist "prayer")

Let me respectfully remind you:
life and death are of supreme importance.

Time swiftly passes by and opportunity is lost.

Each of us should strive to awaken;
Awaken to the present moment!

Take heed,
this night your days are diminished by one.

Do not squander your life.

BILL SCHABERG is the proprietor of Athena Rare Books, a firm specializing in first edition philosophy books published between the 16th and the 20th centuries.

His first book, *The Nietzsche Canon: A Publication History and Bibliography*, was published by the University of Chicago Press in 1995 and seven years later it was translated into German.

Deeply committed to the study of philosophy since college, Schaberg finally had to admit he was never going to find the "answers to life" that he was so diligently searching for within that discipline.

While the ancient philosophers (those original "lovers of wisdom") were primarily trying to discover the best ways for us to live our lives, modern philosophy has veered off into several different specialties (theories of knowledge, language analysis, etc.) that add absolutely nothing to our understanding of how to go about "living well".

It took more than a few years, but Schaberg finally realized that those answers are best found in the experience of others – experiences that have been candidly shared and then attentively heard, accepted and acted upon.

www.ingramcontent.com/pod-product-compliance
Lightning Source LLC
Chambersburg PA
CBHW052307300426
44110CB00035B/2168